I0641983

John Ruskin

Letters Addressed to a College Friend During the Years 1840-1845

John Ruskin

Letters Addressed to a College Friend During the Years 1840-1845

ISBN/EAN: 9783744688024

Printed in Europe, USA, Canada, Australia, Japan

Cover: Foto ©Thomas Meinert / pixelio.de

More available books at **www.hansebooks.com**

LETTERS TO A COLLEGE FRIEND.

LETTERS ADDRESSED
TO A COLLEGE FRIEND
DURING THE YEARS, 1840-1845

BY JOHN RUSKIN.

PUBLISHED BY MACMILLAN & CO.,
NEW YORK; AND GEORGE ALLEN,
LONDON.   MDCCCXCIV.

PUBLISHER'S NOTE

These Letters, together with the Essay ("Was there Death before Adam fell, in other parts of Creation?") are published with Mr. Ruskin's consent; but he is in no way responsible for their arrangement and editing.

June 1894.

CONTENTS

LETTER IV.

[Postmark, Sept. 1, 1840.]

LETTER V.

FRIDAY, 11*th Sept.* [1840?].

LETTER VI.

ROME, *December* 3, 1840.

LETTER VII.

NAPLES, *February* 12, 1841.

LETTER VIII.

VENICE, *May* 16. [*Postmark*, 1841.]

LETTER IX.

LETTER X.

LETTER XI.

LETTER XII.

LETTER XIII.

ESSAY.

LETTER XX.

LETTER XXI.

LETTER XXII.

LETTERS TO A COLLEGE FRIEND

I.

MY DEAR C——

I owe you twenty thousand apologies for not having answered your letter sooner, and countless ones for forgetting your subscription.[1] I do not usually give so much trouble in matters of this kind. I have got into a train of work which leaves me less time than ever—because it is necessary, in order to preserve my eyes, which are weak, that

[1] Post-office shut, couldn't get it; will send it without fail on Monday or Tuesday. (These words were inserted later on.—ED.)

A

I should not use them long at one time on delicate work or subject. Now, while the Academy is open and I am at home, I have to go into town every day to study Turner; this knocks off much of the forenoon. Then I have to write down what I have learned from him. Then I like every fine day to get a little bit of close, hard study from nature; if not out of doors, I bring in a leaf or plant for foreground and draw that. This necessarily leads me to the ascertaining of botanical names and a little microscopic botany. Then I don't like to pass a day without adding to my knowledge of *historical* painting, especially of the early school of Italy: this commonly involves a little bit of work from Raffaelle, and some historical reading, which brings me into the wilderness of the early Italian Republics, and involves me also in ecclesiastical questions, requiring reading of the Fathers (which, however, I have not entered on yet, but am about to do so) and investigation of the religious tenets and feelings of all the branches of the Early Church. Then a little anatomy is indispensable, and much study of technical matters—management of colours, composition, etc. With all this, which would keep my head a great deal too much upon art, I must have a corrective. This comes in the shape of geology, which necessarily leads me into chemistry, and this latter is not a thing to read a bit of now and then, but requires *hard* reading and much learning by rote ; and organic chemistry has made such advances of late that it has become intensely interesting, and draws me on more than it ought. With chemistry and mineralogy, which, though they go together, are totally distinct in the characters (of substances) considered, I am compelled to look at comparative anatomy, especially of fishes, in order to have some acquaintance with the fossil characters of rocks. Then I do not like to give up my Greek altogether, or I should entirely forget it. I, therefore, think myself very wrong if I do not read a little bit of Plato very accurately every day; and reading Plato necessarily involves some thought of something more than language. Finally, as in pursuit of the ancient school of religious painting, I must necessarily go to Italy,[1] it is absolutely necessary that I should know Italian well; so that I have to read

[1] (This reference is probably to the first journey, in the autumn of 1840, into Italy, when he travelled with his parents by the Loire and Riviera to Rome. See "Essay and Letters."—ED.)

a little Tasso every day, which I do with difficulty, never having looked at the language till a month or two back; and I cannot suffer myself entirely to forget my French.

Now, just lay out a day for yourself with these subjects of study, and pre-suppose the necessity of much walking exercise for health, and see if there is much time left for driving about the country; because a day lost with me is lost indeed, for I *cannot* work double tides before or afterwards, owing to the weakness of my eyes. I beg your pardon for being so egotistical, but I was obliged to tell you what I had to do, or you would have thought I was humbugging you.

I am keeping term here, go over to Blenheim as often as I can, where there is a most pure and instructive Raffaelle of his early time—painted at Perugia—I

don't think there is such another in
England. I wish I could see your
woodcarving. Where is East Grins-
stead?

[Letter Unfinished]

II.

SIR,

It is altogether impossible that you can have any moral perception of the value of coins in general, and pence in particular—that you can have formed any distinct ideas of the functions of pence—of their design—and influence on society. You never can have weighed one in your hand—suspended it between your forefinger and thumb—felt that it was an ounce of copper—remembered that it was four farthings—or computed that eleven encores would make it a shilling! a Scotch pound! a piece of silver! a bob!

Have you ever reflected that, in order

to your possession of it, currents of silent lightning have been rushing through the inmost mass of the globe since the foundation of its hills was laid—that chasms have been cloven upwards through its adamant, with the restless electric fire gleaming along their crystalline sides, folded in purple clouds of metallic vapour—that to obtain it for you the sepulchral labour of a thousand arms has penetrated the recesses of the earth, dashed the river from its path, hurled the rock from its seat, sought a way beneath the waves of the deep, heavy sea! For you, night and day, have heaved the dark limbs of the colossal engine—its deep, fierce breath has risen in hot pants to heaven—the crimson furnace has illumined midnight, shaken its fiery hair like meteors among the stars—for you—for you, to abuse and waste the result of their ceaseless labour!

Have you ever sat meditatively in a pastrycook's shop, with no selfish or gluttonous designs upon cheesecake or ice, but to watch the pale faces and sunken eyes which pass lingeringly before the window, and fall upon the consumers of the fruits of earth, half in prayer, and half in accusation? They have no conception of the meaning of the various devices for exciting and pampering the gorged appetite; they never tasted such things in their lives; they are so used to hunger that they do not know what *taste* means! But they gaze as they would on some strange Paradise, when they see the shadows of unknown delights—calls upon senses whose possession they scarcely knew. Have you watched them turning away, sick with famine, weak with desire, with the mild, sorrowful look of subdued reproach at the fixed features and hard brows within (for they are mere children, and have not learned their lessons of rebellion against God and man),—and then reflected that there was but the width and weight of a penny between them and the door? Have you seen some less pitiable urchin, one who has some slight conception of what is meant by the word "tart," pause before the "refuse" chair, at the door, to eye the variegated, black, burned tin-tray, with its arranged square of elliptical raspberry tarts,—the slightest, the very shadow of an amicable adherence existing between them and the tray by means of the rich distillation of crimson, coagulated juice, and their crimped, undulating edge of paste, shaded with

soft brown by the touch of the con-
siderate fire, sinking gradually beneath
the transparent, granular, ruby-tinted
expanse of unimaginably ambrosial jam,
—and considered that a penny would
enable you to sever that juicy connection with the tin, and send the boy away
with bright eyes and elastic step, and
mouth open with wonder, silent with
gratitude, watering with anticipation?
Sir, you have sacrificed half a Good
Samaritanship to insult your friends
with letters of brown paper. I have
half a mind, if I go abroad next
year, to send you from my farthest
point—say, Naples—a box of stones,
3 ft. by 4—by land—carriage *not*
paid.

But, seriously, is that all you can make
of a radish? is that *the* radish, par
excellence—the belle of the season, the

favoured first class, gifted, flavoured, precocious, pungent, unrivalled radish? If it be, all I can say is, it must have been very ill on the road.

Thank you for your sermon about improper jesting: it *was* uncommonly wrong, and I won't do so no more. But what do you mean by "one of us?" Us! Who is "us"? Are you turned editor, or reviewer, or Socialist, or Teetotaller, or Mason, or member of the H. F. Club? or am I to take "us" as a noun collective—representing a class of persons who make their friends talk nonsense whenever they come near them, and pay pence for sending radishes about the country in brown paper?

Seriously, I admire George Herbert above everything, and shall learn "The Church-porch" by heart as soon as I have time; but as for the filthiness, that rests with the bedmakers; and the abusiveness, with the interrogators respecting the faggots;—and Croly may be very profane, but I am afraid he is very true; however, I don't like him as a clergyman, and should like to hear you preach much better.

I have been hard at work with Cocks, getting him to believe in Turner: he is coming steadily round; clever fellow! will soon be all right. He is going up the Nile this winter, to learn to eat raw meat; he'll save in cooks when he comes back, provided they don't cook *him.*

I have seen Newton in town, who is busy giving long names to brass farthings, and putting them in the British Museum. Acland, I had a day's sketching with, at Oxford, and was introduced to Athlone's *fourteen* dogs; he is beginning to think of · parting with some. Nothing new at Oxford, except a Christ Church man's making the Proctor feel the value of *pence* by taking him 480 half-pence by way of a sovereign fine, and remarking to him, as he let go the handkerchief which contained them, that he'd no doubt he would find them all right, if he'd pick them up.

This was done once before, but, by all accounts, not so effectively.

I am reading a little, but dare not do anything by candle-light (for eyes), which upsets me considerably. Pray excite as kind a remembrance of me among your family as you can, when you write home. I hope there is nothing wrong in this letter; tell me if there is, I'll do better next time; only remember that "Hey?" when distinctly interrogative is HEY —not EH, which is an interjection of astonished enquiry. Seriously, don't fancy because I talk lightly, *now* or at other times, that I have no feeling. I am much obliged to you.—Ever truly your friend,

J. RUSKIN.

III.

[*Postmark, July* 31. 1840].

MY DEAR MR. PERFECT ADDITION,

I wish you would not be so very oracular and mysterious in your responses to a plain question. I ask you —with no feeling of indignation whatsoever, but with most marked feelings of curiosity—what you consider yourself, what learned and worshipful society you allude to, when you talk about "us ;" and you tell me this is a highly improper time for asking such a question, and that it would be quite impossible to make me understand anything about your club, and that you are not capable of doing anything but "communicating ideas." I wish in the name of all that's mystical you would do *that*, for you have not communicated anything like an idea to me of what you mean, unless, indeed, from one comparatively intelligible sentence: "You should be a perfect addition, and, therefore, I am bold to say, you should be one of *us*," from which I think I may legitimately conjecture that you consider yourself a "perfect addition" of something or other—that you are a society of "perfect additions," that you are all *quite* perfect additions, and that Mother Earth should have been patted on the head for a good girl when she cast you up; and I suppose you call yourselves the Worshipful Society of Sums — of perfect Sums—or Hums—or something of that kind. But I beg you will be more explanatory next time, for I am not at all

clear about the character of walking
sums any more than Oliver Twist,
when, being suddenly informed that the
" Board was waiting for him," he engaged in that most interesting meditation concerning the probable appearance
of a " live board."

I am very glad to hear you are going
into Cumberland and Derbyshire, though
you have surely been in Cumberland
often before. In Derbyshire take care
to buy no minerals for Mdlle. Emily
(of whose improvement in health I am
very glad to hear), for there is not a
single Derbyshire mineral worth carriage—except, by-the-by, the mineral
Bitumen, elastic asphaltum, of *Castleton*,
of which take her a large piece, for it is
found nowhere else in England, nor,
indeed, in the same way, anywhere.
See Castleton, and the Peak Cavern,

and as many other caverns as you have
time for : they are the only things in
Derbyshire of real interest; and walk
up Dovedale, on a fine day, without expecting much from it. So shall you be
well pleased, particularly if.you glance
at the end of Isaac Walton before
your perambulations ; but if, instead of
Izaak, you take up a guide-book, and
so acquire an echo of "stupendous,
overwhelming, sublime, terrific, and
astonishing," to hum in your ears all
the way, you are done for. There
is nothing above the pretty in any part
of Dovedale.

In Cumberland everybody climbs
Skiddaw—so, of course, you will, if you
can. Ascend the following mountains
also : Helvellyn, Cawsey Pike, Scawfell,
Langdale Pikes, Coniston Man, and the
Pillar of Ennerdale. Do. not miss

Helvellyn on any account, and go up on the *Thirlmere* side, descending to Patterdale if you like, but on no account ascending from Patterdale. I could tell you why if I had room, which I haven't, so *trust* me.

The other peaks are named in the order of their claims to ascent. I think very highly of the view from Cawsey Pike. The Pillar I have not myself ascended, but I know so many places from which it is seen, that the view must be very fine. Take care and don't break your legs or nose on Scawfell: he is an awkward fellow, and you may stick between his loose rocks like Gulliver in the marrow-bone.[1]

When you are at Keswick, and inclined for a long walk, go up by the meadows behind Wallacrag, till you get

[1] (Cf. "Gulliver's Travels."—Ed.)

near its top ; keep straight on the top of the crags towards the head of the lake, catching the views of Derwentwater down the ravines—which, if it be not cloudy, are the finest things in the neighbourhood. When you have passed the top of the crag keep to your right a little, as if you wanted to get down to the shore ; and don't slip, for it is very smooth and steep, and, once off, you would either roll into the lake or get a most disagreeable bruising on a *débris* of crag at the bottom. In a little while you will come to a cart-road : follow it *up* to your left till you come to a stone bridge. Sit down on the rocks above it —or in the water, if you like it better— and eat your lunch ; and when you have done, look about you. For, of all the landscapes I ever saw in my life, I think the view of Derwentwater and Skiddaw

from that spot, with the bridge for a
front object, is the best piece of composition. When you have rested, go up
further still. The cart-road will take you
over the crags above Lodore, on which
you may sit and kick your heels a little
longer ; and mind the ants, for they are
very big. When you have got down to
the stream of Lodore, you will get the
view of the lake through the chasm—
a favourite bit of Southey's, and very
tolerable indeed. Then walk up to
Watendlath, and when you have seen
the Tarn, back to Lodore, and boat it
up to Keswick. I shall not tell you
any more, because I know travellers
always take their own way, whatever
advice they get.

You say, "I have not been guilty
of apologising for delay." Of course
not, for the sin is double : first keeping

a man in suspense, and then wasting
half your penny's worth of paper in
trying to persuade him you couldn't
help it. I don't mean anything *personal*,
it is a most general remark; but, however, between people who call themselves correspondents, I think twelve ·
letters a year—six each—the fewest
that can pass. Consequently, on the
day month after the receipt of a letter,
an apology will become due ; which, if it
does with you, will you have the kind-
ness to cut the apology, and put " B,"
for "bad," at the top of the page ?
whereby I shall know you are sensible
of your delinquency, and we shall both
economise—you in gammon and I in cre-
dulity—of which, considering that you are
going to make me subscribe to the public
dinners of the "Perfect Additions," we
may neither of us have much to spare.

I have not been to see the fossil-child;
because a good, respectable, well-con-
ducted monkey looks so very infantine
when it gets fossilized that, unless I got
the bones out, I mightn't know the
difference. And, again—there is nothing
extraordinary in the skeleton of a human
being found in any of the later rocks,
which are forming at the present
moment. The odd thing would be if
it were not occasionally so.

When we are put into graves, and
get what people call "Christian burial,"
we go to powder in no time, and are
sucked up by the buttercups and daisies
on the top of the graves; and then the
sheep eat us, and we go to assist at our
friends' dinners in the shape of mutton;
or we are diluted with rain-water, and
so go soaking through the earth till
we come out in mineral springs, and

everybody drinks us, and says, "How nice!" But if we are not buried in a respectable way—if we tumble down Niagara, or sink in an Irish bog, or get lost in a coal-hole, or smothered in a sand-pit—the earth takes care of us, and bitumenises, or carbonises, or calcines, or chalcedonises, until we are as durable as rock itself; and then, if we have the luck to get picked up and put in a museum, we may stand there and grin out of the limestone with quite as good a grace as a mammoth or ichthyosaurus.

But although we are found fossil in the rocks now forming, we are *not* in older formations; and if you were to tell me of a fossil child found in clay slate, I would go and look at it—but you won't, in a hurry.

I wrote you immediately because my letter would be too *late*, if you set off beginning of next month, unless I wrote instantly; but I don't intend to write again for two months, for I am reading hard—and you, as you will be wandering and have wet days and nothing to do with yourself, should write at least once in three weeks, I think—but I suppose you don't; however, whatever you do write will be thankfully received. My father and mother send kindest compliments. Remember me in your next letter to all at Twickenham. Believe me,

Ever most truly yours,

J. RUSKIN.

Notwithstanding all this stuff, believe me, I am much obliged for your interest; and, when I have more time, shall be very glad for all encouragement in a path of life which requires all the resolution of a man's character. Wright at Keswick knows more about the country than any other guide ; but don't believe all he tells you about anything but rocks.

IV.

[*Postmark, Sept.* 1, 1840].

DEAR INCOMPREHENSIBLE C——

Of a verity I am sorry you feel my letters overwhelming ; the last *was* rather formidable—I will be more moderate.   As to your going up Helvellyn in rain, it would have ended in your dropping over Striden Edge, and getting set to music by the Poet Laureate, with a dog and a wolf, or some such respectable company, as they did the stocking-manufacturer, or whatever he was, with his sentimental dog—only you hadn't a dog.   Do you remember Scott's lines ?   They all had a touch at him— Wordsworth the best on the whole. Scott had some prettinesses : " How long did'st thou think that his silence was slumber," &c.—but ends always with something about "Catchedicam." They might well say he had no musical ear ; fancy bringing such a heathenish piece of nomenclature as that into a respectable lyric!

Well, I am glad you crossed Styehead ; but what piggish places those lakes are ! If you are an antiquary you must have noticed some connection with a boar, or pig, or sow, in half the names of the country. Did you look for the garnets ? or did I tell you there are plenty of them by the side of the road ? Wastwater— unless on a very fine day—is a very black hole—nothing of a lake ; but I have seen more beautiful atmospheric effects on the Screes above than on any hills in the country. What were you doing at Penrith ? It is not the way to

Derbyshire, nor a very interesting place in itself, except for the view of Saddle-back, as it is vilely called—*Glara-mara*, as the Lake Poets call it—which is monotonous. There is another name which I forget; but it is a noble hill, a glorious hill, an Olympian mountain—but deuced boggy.

I beg the Perfect Addition's pardon; but it *is* deuced, and very uncomfortable walking.

I hope you saw the caverns of Derbyshire thoroughly. They are really interesting, and don't want fine weather; and I hope you didn't tallow your coat-tails. How "precious green" daylight looks when you have been an hour or two holding a candle to dripping, bilious looking stalagmites, and twisting your neck this way and that way to see how very like a whale they are. I can't inquire after *some* places in the Peak. As Winifred Jenkins says, "I can't pollewt my pen "—though, by-the-bye, you may find every piece of coarseness coined in the United Kingdom in that book. I cannot, for the life of me, understand the feelings of men of magnificent wit and intellect, like Smollett and Fielding, when I see them gloating over and licking their chops over nastiness, like hungry dogs over ordure; founding one half of the laughable matter of their volumes in innuendoes of abomination. Not that I think, as many people do, they are bad books; for I don't think these pieces of open filth are in reality injurious to the mind, or, at least, *as* injurious as corrupt sentiment and disguised immorality, such as you get sometimes in Bulwer and men of his school. But I cannot

understand the taste. I can't imagine
why men who have real wit at their
command should *perfume* it as they do.

Have you any commands for Naples?
for I hope to be there before Christmas ; we intend to start for Boulogne
on Tuesday fortnight, and go through
Normandy and Auvergne leisurely, so
to Marseilles and Genoa—very pleasant,
isn't it? I have thrown up reading
altogether—partly for eyes, partly because a little more blood came from
my chest the other night, and Sir James
Clarke insists on it. I hope to bring
home quantities of sketches — fresh
health—and a quantity of *nonchalance* as
to Oxford examinations.

I have come to the conclusion that
Aristotle was a muddle-head. If you
would like to know why, I will tell you
in my next. You may depend upon it,

the people who cry him up don't understand a word of him. The fellow who has edited my edition has written such prodigious nonsense by way of notes, that I take up the "Ethics" when I want a laugh, as I would Molière. I don't mean to say that Aristotle was not what Lord Verisopht[1] considered Shakespeare, "a clayver man." I simply mean to say he has muddled himself, and many as clear heads as his own into the bargain. If they read him as they ought at the University—that is, telling the student to find out what was nonsense and what was falsehood, and learn the rest by heart — no *very* heavy task—they would do good, for what *is* good of the "Ethics" is *very* good; but as they do at present— reading as if it were all gospel—I am

[1] (Cf. " Nicholas Nickleby."—ED.)

certain it does as much harm as good.

If I can get over to Richmond before I start I shall call at Twickenham, and enquire if I can bring over any little tiny kickshaw of antiquity from Italy for the top of your filigree cabinet, or the inside of Mdlle. Emily's more philosophical and respectable one; but if I am not heard of within that time, apologise for me, as I have much to do preparing suddenly for a winter in Italy.

I have thrown up St. James Street, so direct to Herne Hill, near Dulwich, London; and mind this—put a cross as big as *that*[1] opposite the stamp, for as I receive a quantity of rubbish-letters now—and don't intend to pay postage

[1] (The cross, being merely a rough scrawl, is not reproduced.—ED.)

for nothing—any letters *un*crossed will
not be forwarded to me.

I mean by opposite, the stamp on
the other side of the direction.—Ever
very truly yours,

J. RUSKIN.

V

FRIDAY, 11*th* *Sept.* [1840?].

DEAR C——

When I get once abroad I shall have so much generalising and sketching, that I shall be unable to write many letters, so I put you in debt before starting. First, to say that you ought to congratulate yourself on my orthography—it was lucky I didn't put warming-pan. Secondly, that you would not have been surprised at this escapade of mine had you heard Sir J. Clarke's positive " Sir, if you go on till October you'll get your death before you get your degree—" under which circumstances, of course, I care very little about Dean or anyone else. I simply send them fine medical certificates, lock up my books, and start. Thirdly, to assure you your Nap. soap shall be taken great care of. Fourthly, to thank your brother for his notice. Fifthly, to tell you to blow up your spectacle-maker, and not me, for the deficiency of Gothic work on the Carlisle house ; and sixthly, to put down a few remarks—in serious deprecation of your worship's indigna-tion—which, as you are drawing a good deal from nature, may perhaps be of some interest to you ; and if you don't take the trouble to read them, it will do *me* good to arrange them and put them down.

The object of high art is to address the feelings *through* the intellect. It will not do to address the feelings, unless it be through this medium—still less, to address the intellect alone.

Consequently the mere conveying of a certain quantity of technical knowledge respecting any given scene can never be the object of art. Its aim is not to tell me how many bricks there are in a wall, nor how many posts in a fence, but to convey as much as possible the general emotions arising out of the real scene into the spectator's mind.

Whether these emotions are conveyed by the same *means* signifies little, but they must be the same *emotions ;* and I do not mean merely a sensation of sublimity, or beauty, or generality of any kind, but the particular feeling and character of the place,—the pervading spirit, with as much of detail as is consistent with it. Have you not sometimes wondered why, if the object of art be mere servility of imitation of nature, there were as many *styles* as there were great artists? The true reason is that each great artist conveys to you, not so much the scene, as the impression of the scene, on his own originality of mind. Ruysdael looks to nature for her freshness and purity,—Rubens for her glory of colour,—Poussin for her tumult,—Salvator for her energy,—Claude for her peace,—Turner (I rise to a climax) for her mystery and divinity.

And each of these throw out of their studies from nature whatever has a tendency to destroy purity, or colour, or energy, or peace, or mystery.

Now, when you sit down to sketch from nature you are not to *compose* a scene—as you insinuate against me— from materials before you. Still less are you to count stones, or measure angles. You are to imbue your mind with the peculiar spirit of the place. (If it has none, it is not worth sketching.) You are to give this spirit, at all risks, by any means; and if it depends upon accessories which you cannot represent truly, you must *lie* up to them in some way or another, always preserving as much technicality as you have time for, and as is in harmony with your general intention.

If you ask any portrait-painter how he gets his likeness, he will tell you, it is not by attention to the form of particular features—the technicality of countenance—but by aiming first at the marked expression of the individual *character*, then touching in the features over this.

Now, for instance, in my Coniston cottage,[1] it happened, from the point where I sat, that I could not see an

[1] (Cf. " Poetry of Architecture."—ED.)

inch of mountain over the trees. I have, nevertheless, put in the whole mass of the Old Man—why? Because the eye, in reality, falls on that cottage when it is full of the forms and feeling of mountain scenery, and judges by comparison with it; it feels its peculiar beauty only as a *mountain* cottage, and can return to a mountain by turning an eighth of the compass. But I cannot turn you in a single sketch; I cannot give you the feeling that it is a bit of mountain scenery, without giving you a single touch of mountain blue. I am, therefore, in conscience, telling less of a lie by raising the Old Man a thousand feet, than by giving to the eye the idea of a lowland cottage.

Another character of this cottage is seclusion. The turnpike road was a violation of this; I turned it out of my way, or, rather, did what you might have done—leaped the wall, and sketched with my back to it.

Well, if you have time to turn over the subject in your mind, I think you will find some truth in these principles ; and you will soon emancipate yourself from any idea that artists' sketches are to be mere camera-lucidas, mere transcripts of mechanism and measurement. It is of no consequence to any mortal that there is a cottage eighteen feet high by twenty-five broad, with a wall three bricks thick, and trees thirty years old and eighteeen inches round ; but it is— or may be—of some interest to know that there is a piece of secluded cottage feeling by Coniston Water, or that such and such a character is peculiar to the cottages of the Lakes.

As for writing, I do not know exactly

where I am going ; but if you write to
Herne Hill, with a cross, your letters
will always be forwarded.

I forgot to say that I think you
deserve great credit for finding the
places at all, especially Carlisle ; it shows
you a use of *spouts*, which I suppose is
new to you.

And I do not mean to advocate
violent innovation where the subject is
entirely architectural. The Gothic work
is on the house—'pon honour!—but it
is so black and smoky, that I do not
wonder at your not making it out. And
there is a good medium. One *side* of
Prout's drawings is generally sheer composition ; this is going too far for a man
who can't compose. Turner is very faithful, but he is the only man alive who
can be faithful and yet preserve character ; and you know even *he* thinks

nothing of cutting an island out of the Thames when it is in his way.

When the day of publication comes, a Friendship's Offering[1] will be sent to Twickenham, as I shall leave orders with publisher, and crave you to allow it room in your bookcase, as there is much lucubration of mine therein.

Write me as often as you can.—Ever very truly yours,

J. RUSKIN.

I am afraid I shall be unable to get to Twickenham : it is heavy work preparing in a week or two for a year abroad.

[1] (The volume for 1841 contained " The Tears of Psammenitus," " The Two Paths," " The Old Water-wheel," " Farewell!" " The Departed Light," and " Agonia." Cf. " Poems of John Ruskin," published in complete form in 1891.—ED.)

VI.

Dear C——

Since I started, in a very blowy
day, from Dover, I have sent off some
dozen of diaries to people on post paper,
for which I have not as yet got a grain
of thanks, and I have received two
letters from you, whom I have hitherto
neglected, for which I infinitely thank
you; for there are few things more
melancholy than jostling through a set
of black-whiskered blackguards, every
one of whom look as if they would
enjoy putting you in a pie and eating
you—a group of strange, foreign, heathenish faces and dresses—up to the
window of the post-office, and turning

back into the crowd without one single witness of memory from England.

One never feels so far from home as in the first pause of meditation upon possible accidents to the mail. I am quite tired of telling people what I have been about—which, by-the-by, is not always the most interesting topic to the reader, unless he be one's particular friend, though I shall venture upon it with *you*, after refreshing myself with a little chat about the water-colour society.

You ask about a water-colour master, with some little scruple about time and expense. I am quite certain that neither time nor expense, within certain limits, can be employed with greater certainty of redounding in the end to your own usefulness and happiness than in raising your feeling and taste—that

is, your perception of the Beautiful.
For the end of study in us who are not
to be artists is not to be able to bring
home from Wales or Derbyshire outlines of cottages or mill-wheels enough
to occupy the quarter of an hour before
dinner with chit-chat, but to receive,
what I am persuaded God means to
be the *second* source of happiness to
man—the impression of that mystery
which, in our total ignorance of its
nature, we call "beauty." It is the
Θεωρία of Aristotle; and when purely
founded—which it cannot be without
some care and some study—will most
certainly last us when every other
passion has passed away into the mist
of extreme old age, with unabated
power; and, in all probability, will retain
its influence in all stages of existence
of which a pure spirit is capable. That

study of all art is nothing but the cultivation of this feeling for the beautiful, and knowledge of its principles, you either know, or will know very soon. Still, it is not to be acquired by any lessons from even the highest masters; it depends much more, as you must feel, on your own constant watchfulness of Nature and love of her. All that the master does in general—whatever his system of *talking* may be—is to awake your *attention* to facts. The rest is all habit and mechanism, and it is always in your power to cultivate your powers of attention yourself. But if you take lessons at all, take them from the best. One lesson from them, which will cost you a guinea, is worth three from others, which will cost you ten shillings each. The choice lies between three—Harding, De Wint, and Cox.

I will tell you what I know of each, and then you can choose.

Harding is indisputably the highest and most accomplished landscape artist who gives lessons in England at the present day, but he will not teach you *colouring ;* he despises it himself, and will not allow it in you. A day or two before I started I was with him about some sketching questions, and he took out a portfolio of *coloured* sketches he had just made in Scotland, for me to look over. I was much delighted with their magnificent precision of tone. "I am glad of that," said Harding, "for they are the first sketches in *colour* I ever made in my life."

This from one of the first landscape masters of England was a little surprising. The fact is, Harding rests everything upon form and light and

D

shade; and the first thing he will do with you, and does with everybody, will be to take the brush out of your fingers and put a piece of chalk in, and say, " Draw." And he will keep you drawing, if you obey him, till you can draw as well as he can, before he will give you a brush. In the main, he is quite right ; form is almost everything.

Turner, the great ruler, studies every one of his pictures in light and shade before he thinks of colour ; and if you once saw such a chalk sketch as I did the other day in Florence, hanging up over Michael Angelo's own old slippers, in his own old house,—finished like an engraving, in parts, all by his own hand,—I don't think you would ever touch colour more.

At any rate, for a person who has much time, Harding's system is the right and the only true one. But as, unluckily, all the time which probably you will have to spare for these ten years would hardly raise you up to Harding's mark for beginning in colour, and as it is very agreeable to be able to put down a striking tint or two from Nature, even if it be not forwarding you by the straight road to excellence, you must get some other master.

De Wint is Harding's direct contrary, in all respects. He despises form, because he cannot draw a straight line, and will tell you, "Never mind your drawing, but take plenty of colour on your brush, and lay it on very thick." He despises all rules of composition, hates Old Masters and humbug—synonymous terms with him—never was abroad in his life, never sketches anything but pigstyes and haystacks, and is a thorough-going John Bull of an artist in all respects. But, to make amends for all this, he is a most ardent lover of *truth* —hardly ever paints except from nature, attends constantly and effectually to colour and tone, and produces sketches of such miraculous truth of atmosphere, colour and light, that half an hour's work of his, from nature, has fetched its fifty guineas, and a parcel of his sketches has often been exchanged for a Turner.

I think, myself, he is just your man, especially as he will allow you to make a mess of your colour-box, which I know you like ; but all that he can do for you will be to teach you to make a forcible sketch of an atmospheric effect on simple objects ; he smothers all detail, and his trees are as like cabbages as anything else.

Cox is a much more agreeable artist,

as to results, than De Wint, and a much simpler one than Harding. De Wint is always true, always wonderful, and always ugly. Cox is neither so true, nor so powerful, but his sketch is twenty times more beautiful.

He is a man of dew: his sketches breathe of morning air, and his grass would wet your feet through, if you were to walk on it in Hoby's best. His mountains are melting with soft shadows, and his clouds at once so clear and so vaporous, so craggy, and so æthereal, that you expect to see them dissolve before you. But with all this he has neither the truth of De Wint nor the science of Harding : he is a man of less forcible conception than the one, of less cultivated knowledge than the other. He is a mannerist, and all his pupils become merely inferior Coxes. What

his mode of teaching is I do not know
from experience; but I believe, from
what I have heard and seen of his pupils,
that it is rather instruction in mechanical
laying on of colour, and communication
of certain tricks, touches, and tints,—
peculiarly his own,—than any general
explanation of principles of art. All his
pupils become *clever*, but never original,
and always smell of him to the corners
of their paper.

I think myself De Wint is your man;
for the ardent love of truth which is his
chief characteristic he always communi-
cates, and it is invaluable. For you
may get Harding's " Use of the Lead-
pencil," in which you have much of his
knowledge conveniently arranged; and,
if you do not boggle at it because it
professes to be for beginners, which all
amateurs almost are, you will find it

invaluable, a thing to be learnt by heart.

But, above all, let me beseech you, whenever you see a stained engraving in a pawnbroker's window with the four letters J.M.W.T. at the left-hand corner, buy it; get the old annuals, which are to be had for nothing almost; Heath's " Landscape " and others, where you are sure of three or four delicate plates from him—Turner; get Rogers' " Italy " and " Poems," they are getting cheap (I think you have the " Italy "); and the " Rivers of France," in which you get sixty engravings for a sovereign; and take them to bed with you, and look at them before you go to sleep, till you dream of them; and when you are reading and come to anything that you want to refer to often, put a little Turner in to keep the place, that your eye may fall on it whenever you

open.   He is the epitome of all art, the
concentration of all power ; there is nothing that ever artist was celebrated for,
that he cannot do better than the most
celebrated. He seems to have seen everything, remembered everything, spiritual-
ised everything in the visible world ;
there is nothing he has not done, nothing
that he dares not do ; when he dies, there
will be more of nature and her mysteries
forgotten in one sob, than will be learnt
again by the eyes of a generation.

However, if I get to Turner I shall
get prosy, and I suppose you have had
enough of the brush for one letter ; so
I shall leave the discussion, in which
you beat so courteous and cowardly
a retreat, unpursued at present,—only
begging you not to suppose that anything I have just said about *truth*
militates against my former positions,

and also to excuse any flippancy or too decisive expression I may fall into in talking of these things, partly from hurry and partly from zeal; for I cannot say "I think" and "it seems to me" perpetually in a letter. It takes both time and room to be modest on paper, and I have neither to spare.

Now for a bit of diary.

First I went to Rouen—no, before that, to Neuchâtel, and had some cheese —beatific! Then to Rouen, and caught a cold. Then to Chartres, and got well again. I wish you had seen "La Vierge Noire," the presiding deity of Chartres Cathedral—a little black lady (with a black baby) in a bright white muslin frock, and seven or eight silk petticoats, and a crown of little spiky stars, and a little reticule on her arm, and pink satin *beaux* on her wrists, and a priest perpetually saying his prayers to her, and changing her petticoats, and everybody in the town bringing her votive pin-cushions—"On a beaucoup de dévotion pour elle," said the waiter. Then to Orleans, racing a carter all the way;—thank heaven! till some patriotic Frenchman burns down the Cathedral of Orleans, our National Gallery is *not* the vilest piece of architecture in Europe. Then to Blois—such a barracks of buggy bedrooms, with little holes and passages and panels between, where people used to be poisoned and stabbed—delicious! Then to Amboise,—the scene of the "Broken Chain,"[1]—and had some mutton chops. Then to Tours, and saw the house of Tristan l'Hermite, all decorated with effigies of different sized ropes,—and a church!! I should like

[1] (Cf. "Poems of John Ruskin."—ED.)

excessively to see your High Church principles driven in a diligence into St. Julien—a noble cathedral turned into a coachhouse; horses stabled in the aisles; hay and straw crammed into the Gothic tracery, which makes a capital rack; diligences standing all up the choir and transepts, and the columns pasted over with "AVIS DU DÉPART,"&c. Then to Aubusson, and made some carpet. Then to Clermont, and bought some petrified thistledown. Then to Le Puy, and lost our way. Then to St. Etienne, and ran against a diligence. Then to Vaucluse, and saw the legitimate bonâ fide portraits of Petrarch and Laura— Petrarch like a butcher playing Julius Cæsar at Astley's, Laura with pink eyes and a hatchet nose. It is, however, recorded in [1]   that the inn of

[1] (Two words undecipherable.—Ed.)

Petrarch and Laura gives some of the best dinners on the Continent, which makes it worth going. Then to Aix, and got nearly blown away by the *Bise*. Then to Nice, where there is a glorious military Mass on Sunday morning, and a shady English service where the people go to show their bonnets on Sunday forenoon, and a splendid military band on Sunday evening—long live the King of Sardinia! Then to Genoa, and got some velvet. Then to Carrara, and bought two people whom I took for Adam and Eve, but everybody else says they are Bacchus and Ariadne—*tant mieux*. Carrara is a nice place. Imagine a range of noble mountains from 5000 to 7000 feet high, terminating in jagged and inaccessible peaks, on whose bases, fourteen miles off, you can just discern two little white chips,

as if a cannon ball had grazed the hills.
These, as you get nearer, increase in
apparent size till, after a walk over an
old Roman road paved with marble,
you arrive at the lowest, which you find
to be a group of seven or eight quarries,
each the size of the great one on Head-
ingdon, and the last deep and large, in
rocks of lump-sugar—exquisite, snow-
white, stainless marble—out of whose
dead mass life is leaping day by day
into every palace of Europe: all the
roads covered with snowy debris, and
the torrent leaping over blocks of bright,
neglected alabaster—it is a glorious
place! Then to Pisa, and got giddy
on its nasty squinting tower. Then to
Florence, which was the most awful
thing I ever encountered in the way
of a disappointment ; and, at last, here we
are, among brick-dust and bad Latin

ad nauseam. I have not made up my
mind about St. Peter's : there is certainly
a great deal too much light in it, which
destroys size ; it is kept a little too
clean, and the bright colours of its
invaluable marbles tell gaudily, and the
roof is ugly, merely a great basket of
golden wickerwork ; but if you go into
its details, and examine its colossal pieces
of sculpture which gleam through every
shadow, the thorough *get up* of the
whole, the going the *whole hog*, the
inimitable, unimaginable art displayed
into every corner and hole, the concentration of human intellect and of the
rarest and most beautiful materials that
God has given for it to work with,
unite to raise such feelings as we can
have only once or twice in our lives.
The value of intellect and material con-
centrated in one of the minor chapels of

St. Peter's would have built Canterbury
or York.

I have been much pleased with the
Vatican, which takes about an hour's
quick walk to get you through from
one end to the other, passing a statue
for every second,—and such statues! I
never knew what sculpture meant before.
Above all I was surprised at the extraordinary differences between the usual
casts and copies of the Laocoon and
Apollo (and Venus at Florence) and the
originals. Of course the copyers cannot
take *casts* off the actual statuary, and are
obliged to do it by eye; or they try
to improve them or something, I don't
know what—but, instead of coming to
the Belvidere, as to a known hackneyed
form, I started at it as if I had never
seen it in my life. And the Venus,
usually in her casts a foolish little

schoolgirl, is one of the purest and
most elevated incarnations of woman
conceivable. As for ancient Rome, it
is a nasty, rubbishy, dirty hole—I hate
it. If it were all new, and set up again
at Birmingham, not a soul would care
twopence for it.

As for myself, I am better, though
my eyes are still weak; nothing but a
little roughness left of my affection of
chest; and my eyes are better, though,
as you may imagine, they have had a
great deal to try them. I am delighted
by Acland's success at Oxford—many
thanks for your other news. My father
and mother send their best thanks for
your remembrances and kind regards.
I hope to be at Naples in about a
month—after Christmas, that is—and
won't forget your soap. If I find anything particularly well formed from

Vesuvius, I will bring it for Mdlle. Emily, of whose improved health I was delighted to hear. Pray remember me most kindly to all your family. I have not answered your conversation about the Church, because I sympathise completely in all you say, and I don't see the use of answering unless you have to contradict something or somebody. What a stupid thing conversation would be without contradiction ! I wish you would come and preach here on the Continent ; there are more clergymen in England than people will listen to. Here they are more wanted than among South Sea islands, and many poor isolated curates keeping up a heavy struggle, with no money and few hearers, and a stable for a church.— Ever, dear C——, most truly yours,

J. RUSKIN.

E

VII

NAPLES, *February* 12, 1841.

Positively, my dear C——, you are a capital correspondent. It is a hopeless thing sending off a letter which will take twenty days to go, to a correspondent who will take two months to answer. I don't think your "B." was necessary this time : you could not have been a calendar month silent, and I am excessively obliged to you. I don't know what I should do this nasty wet day, if I had not your epistle to answer.

I do wish most sincerely that we could get associated in our duties in some way or other, for I shall not be fit for much myself, except taking the tea-making business off your hands.

The least speaking or reading makes me hoarse, and if I go on for a quarter of an hour my throat gets irritated and makes me cough; so how I am to preach I cannot tell. I have had a slight return of the blood from my chest here—less than ever, but still it keeps me to cautionary measures, which are an infernal bore when you are among hills. I only wish I *could* smile at grief on the top of a rock; but I am obliged to stay at the bottom, or take the ladylike expedient of a *chaise à porteur;* and you know, if you once get me into that, with the blinds up, you may send me wherever you like,—and a fig for the vicar, as somebody remarks to the Lady of the Lake.

The worst of it is, it checks one in taking up any design that requires time. I have begun a work of some labour[1] which would take me several years to complete; but I cannot read for it, and do not know how many years I may have for it. I don't know if I shall even be able to get my degree; and so I remain in a jog-trot, sufficient-for-the-day style of occupation—lounging, planless, undecided, and uncomfortable, except when I can get out to sketch— my chief enjoyment. I am beginning to consider the present as the only available time, and in that humour it is impossible to work at anything dry or laborious or useful. I spend my days in a search after present amusement, because I have not spirit enough to labour in the attainment of what I

[1] (" Modern Painters."—ED.)

may not have future strength to attain; and yet am restless under the sensation of days perpetually lost and employment perpetually vain.

If I could even avail myself of the opportunities of amusement about me I should not care, for they are all instructive in their way; but I cannot draw more than an hour or two in the day, for my eyes, nor—but I suppose I have told you all my cannots before—*n'importe.*

I have been thinking a little more of your "perfect additions" lately; and I dare say there is a great deal of comfort in religious matters, for people like an old gentleman who was giving me a sketch of his life, as we came out of church yesterday, concluding with : " I'm greatly blessed! highly favoured! hale and hearty of my age !—and *such* peace !

such views of divine things! amazin'!"
But, do you know, I think a fiat of
general annihilation would be a far more
comfortable thing for mankind in general than the contest between Satan and
St. Michael, with 10 to 1 on the devil.
I had rather, myself, be sure of rest
than know I was to sing for ever—with
great odds it was to be on the wrong
side of my mouth.

I don't mean to jest upon the matter,
nor to shock you; but those texts about
the straight (*sic*) gate are awkward
things for the public.

Many—infinite, as you say—thanks
for your notice of my poems; only that
was a neat way of beginning a letter,
which was to explode *my infinities*
altogether. I am the more obliged
because it is nearly impossible to get
any quiet or candid criticism from

anyone. I have a great deal said about the "brilliant effusions of my pen" by ladies—who never read, and couldn't have understood, a word of them—and I have received occasional flagellations from an offended gazette; but, happening to know some matters behind the scenes, I have long ceased even to read public criticisms; and few friends venture; so I thank you again for really reading them, and still more for telling me your opinion; and I will thank you still more if you will hear what I can say in my justification with respect to the particular faults you mention; for, depend on it, people who write verses are like mankind in their morality: they will allow themselves at once to be sinners in the general way, but are always prepared with excuses when you name a particular sin.

I think you have not sufficiently considered that "Psammy"[1] is throughout a *speech*, a dramatic piece—not a poem in which the *author* professes to be speaking. If you have ever felt the dreamy confusion, the delirious weight of *intellectual* pain consequent on sudden and violent sorrow, you would not expect a man in Psammenitus's situation to be distinct in a single idea or expression. In such circumstances all thought becomes a sensation, and all sensation becomes *sight;* and the kingdoms of the several senses are dashed into such anarchy in a moment that they invade and dethrone each other; the thoughts become rapid and involuntary, taking almost a visible form; and every sensation takes a delirious

[1] ("The Tears of Psammenitus." Cf. "Poems of John Ruskin."—ED.)

hold of the brain, rushing there from
every part of the body, and confusing
and exciting its powers at the same
time ; all the faculties are in an energetic, but a diseased and involuntary,
state of action—the memory, for instance
becomes capable of grasping years of
events in a moment, but has no power
over itself, could not seize at its own
wish the circumstances of an instant
ago—all is forced upon it.

It is this state of mind which I particularly aimed at depicting in the "Psammenitus," and I ought to have succeeded, for
the thing was written in two hours as
a relief from strong and painful excite-
ment. The choice of subject, I agree
with you, is wrong ; but I wrote this,
and five or six other pieces, as illustrations of Herodotus, partly because I
thought there was a great deal of the

picturesque lying neglected in this historian, and partly to fix the history in my mind while I read it. " The Scythian Grave," " The Scythian Banquet-song," " The Scythian Guest," "Aristodemus at Platea," "The Last Song of Arion,"[1] &c., were all written with this intention.

Now, as you say, to come to particulars : *entre nous*, you are not quite up to our dodge of great value in matters of criticism. You should never *actually* come to particulars, for authors are very apt to come down upon you with "authorities"—there being an authority for almost every absurdity that can be committed either in literary or practical matters. You should only *say* you are going to particularise ; then extract a portion of some twenty lines which you conceive the writer supposes

[1] (Cf. " The Poems of John Ruskin."—Ed.)

" fine "—put twenty notes of interroga-
tion and admiration alternately all down
at the end of the lines—and then ask the
author point blank "what he means by
the whole passage." If that doesn't non-
plus him I don't know what will. But
whereas you condescend to particularise
bonâ fide, I cannot help endeavouring to
get myself out of the scrape.

You quarrel first with the "bars" of
darkness. Now, my dear fellow, I said
bars, I didn't say *crow*bars ; and if, when
I intend you to lie like a good tractable
wild beast, with the shadow of your bars
between you and the light, you are to
pitch them at my head like a Cornish
miner—it is *I* who ought to cry "Hold!"

I do seriously maintain that, mono-
syllable, dissyllable, or polysyllable,
there is not another word in the English language so effectively expressive

of partial, prolonged, parallel shade as
" bars."

What would you say? " Streaks "?
A streak is properly applied only to a
line which is thin and drawn out—like
the delineations in beer on a public-
house table, *par exemple.* "Stripes"?
That smells of wild cat and improper
servants. " Lines"? A line is length
without breadth. " Parallelograms "?
Slightly unpoetical, I think—but if you
can bring it into the verse, do, by all
means. So that actually, "bar" is the
only word I could have used with any
propriety. But if you particularly desire to suppose farther that Psammenitus
had a very unpleasant headache, and
that every shadow that past left a sensation of his brains being made into Yorkshire pudding by self-acting rolling-pins,
I have not the slightest objection to

such an interpretation—nay, I think the beauty of the expression must be enhanced by its comprehensiveness.

Next you proceed, or go back rather, to the " keen pain " of the line before, and you ask me " Who ever heard of *cold* pain ? "—may I ask you in return who ever heard of *hot* shadows ?   A shadow is a very common metaphor for sorrow. If a shadow is cool—if you don't put very much more cobalt than Indian-red into them—you will find your drawing look very unpleasant.   And, moreover, as shadow is a *keen* thing, it has a cutting edge, which you can only get with a very full brush, as you must very well know.   And, letting the shadows alone, I think I may prove that all *sorrow*, if unmixed with feelings of anger or revenge, is *cold*.   Did you ever hear of anybody who was burying their relations

one after another, remarking that it was
" warm work"?   Did you ever yourself
when you had lost a friend—if it were
but a dog—feel the warmer for it?   On
the contrary, the cry of the bereaved
is *always* " Poor Tom's a-cold."[1]

The feeling in its first acuteness
might perhaps be metaphorically styled
" burning "—just as the existence of cold
has the same effect and sensation as the
extreme of heat ; but it is always a
chill, an icy feeling about the heart,
which cloak nor fire will never banish
more.   What is the common metaphor
for the desolation of a bereaved age ?
Winter.   Even *you*, in your " All hot—
sugar and brandy " style, would not
talk of a man's being in the dog-days
of his life when he had lost everyone
who cared for him.   And although *some*

[1] (Cf. " King Lear."—ED.)

mental pain—rage, jealousy, envy, revenge, &c.—may be burning, I do not
intend the mind of Psammenitus to be
touched by any of these at this instant.
The vision of his sons, led to death, is
passing before his eyes. He has but
one feeling—that the forms are vanishing
for ever; he remembers not the cause,
he only knows that each walks hand in
hand with death; and their shadows
as they pass fall, each with the bitter,
irrevocable *chill* that all the suns of
heaven can never break. I have tried,
in this line, to express the confusion of
the senses by which they are felt at
once cold to the heart, quivering to the
eye, and keen to the brain.

Verily, I think it is a little too bad to
begin a second sheet of egotism on you.
But, after all, I think it is pleasanter
to be discussing some real subject of

interest, like that suggested by the remarks of yours—which I have yet to answer—than to tell you where I was when you were writing to me—that when it was a soft rain with you it was a soft sun with me. And I was sitting above the grotto of Posilipo, sketching a ruined palace by a rocky shore, as foreground to the sweeping line of the blue bay and bright city of Naples, and doing all I could—with Chinese white—to come up to the dazzling brightness of the drift of vapour—call it not smoke—floating from the lips of Vesuvius.[1]

I am getting as fond of Vesuvius as of a human creature; and have been very happy to-day sauntering through the frescoed chambers of Pompeii, with a sun as bright upon their azures as ever

[1] (See the illustration, "Bay of Naples, 1841," facing p. 142 of " The Poetry of Architecture."—ED.)

rejoiced with the rejoicing of those
whom they have lost.

But—to go back to Psammy—I think
I have only one more particular objection to answer. You say, do not I
mean "forgive," instead of "forget, the
thoughts of him," &c.? Now, the third
line after this passage is: "No tear—
Hath quenched the *curse* within mine
eyes." Is this very like forgiveness?
I merely mean the expression to stand
for a gentlemanlike apology on the part
of Psammy, for keeping King C.'s mes-
senger waiting while he was rigmaroling
about red air, and white hair. Suddenly he recollects himself: "Dear me,
I quite forgot! I beg pardon! What
was it Cambyses was *thinking* about
me?"

Now, I think, as far as Psammenitus
goes, I have got pretty well out of the

scrape, if you will accept the above apology for its obscurity. But as I suppose you intend to refer in some degree to the other poems, I must come to generals.

You say that infinity of conception ought to belong only to religion. Granted. But what object or sensation in earth or heaven has not religion in it—that is, has not something to do with God, and therefore with both infinity and mystery? You cannot banish infinity from space or time, nor mystery from every motion of your body, every pulse of your heart, every exertion of mental energy? How can you speak, when you have no knowledge, and keep clear of mystery? and how far in any subject does the highest human knowledge extend? Will you undertake to convey to another person a perfectly distinct idea of any single simple emotion passing in your own heart?

You cannot—you cannot fathom it yourself—you have no actual expression for the simple idea, and are compelled to have instant recourse to metaphor.

You can say, for instance, you feel cold, or warm, at the heart; you feel depressed, delighted, dark, bright: are any of these expressions competent to illustrate the *whole* feeling? If you try to reach it you must heap on metaphor after metaphor, and image after image, and you will feel that the most mysterious touch nearest and reach highest, but none will come up to the truth. In short, if you banish obscurity from your language you banish all description of human emotion, beyond such simple notions as that your hero is in a fury or a fright. For all human emotions are obscure, mysterious in their source, their operation, their nature; and how possibly can the *picture* of a mystery be less than a mystery?

But, farther—were it possible, it is not desirable to banish all obscurity from poetry. If the mind is delighted in the attainment of a new idea, its delight is increased tenfold if it be obtained by its own exertion—if it has arisen apparently from its own depths.

The object in all *art* is not to *inform* but to *suggest*, not to add to the knowledge but to kindle the imagination. He is the best poet who can by the fewest words touch the greatest number of secret chords of thought in his reader's own mind, and set *them* to work in their own way. I will take a simple instance in epithet. Byron begins

something or other [1]—"Tis midnight:
on the mountains brown—The pale
round moon shines deeply down."
Now the first eleven words are not
poetry, except by their measure and
preparation for rhyme; they are simple
information, which might just as well
have been given in prose—it *is* prose, in
fact: It is twelve o'clock—the moon is
pale—it is round—it is shining on
brown mountains.

Any fool, who had seen it, could tell
us all that. At last comes the poetry,
in the single epithet, "deeply." Had
he said "softly" or "brightly" it would
still have been simple information.

But of all the readers of that couplet,
probably not two received exactly the
same impression from the "deeply,"
and yet received more from that than

[1] ("The Siege of Corinth."—ED.)

from all the rest together. Some will refer the expression to the fall of the steep beams, and plunge down with them from rock to rock into the woody darkness of the cloven ravines, down to the undermost pool of eddying black water, whose echo is lost among their leafage ; others will think of the deep heaven, the silent sea, that is drinking the light into its infinity ; others of the deep *feeling* of the pure light, of the thousand memories and emotions that rise out of their rest, and are seen white and cold in its rays. This is the reason of the power of the single epithet, and this is its *mystery*.

Where it is thus desired, as in almost all good poetry it is, that the reader should work out much for himself, it becomes necessary to keep his mind in a peculiar temper, adapted for the exercise of the imagination : to do this, rhyme and rhythm are introduced, as melody, to assist the fancy, and bring the whole mind into an elevated and yet soothed spirituality. Where nothing is to be left to the imagination, where all is to be told downright, this is totally unnecessary : we can receive plain facts in any temper.

Now, in all art, whatever is not useful is detrimental. Rhyme and rhythm are, therefore, thoroughly injurious where there is no mystery, when there is not some undermeaning, some repressed feeling ; and thus, in five-sixths of Scott's poetry, as it is called, the metre is an absolute excrescence, the rhythm degenerates into childish jingle, and the rhyme into unseemly fetters to yoke the convicted verses together.

" Rokeby," had it been written in his

own noble prose style, would have been one of his very first-raters ; at present, it is neglected even by his most ardent admirers. And thus, not only is obscurity necessary to poetry, it is the only apology for writing it.

My space is diminishing so fast that I cannot say what I would of particular men, or I think I could show you in any real poet, Shakspeare, Wordsworth, Coleridge, Shelley, Byron, Spenser, G. Herbert, Elizabeth Barrett—whom you choose—that their finest passages never *can* be fathomed in a minute, or in ten minutes, or exhausted in as many years. But this I can say, that if you sit down to read poetry with merely the wish to be amused, without a willingness to take some pains to work out the secret meanings, without a desire to sympathise with, and yield to, the prevailing spirit of the writer, you had better keep to prose : for no poetry is worth reading which is not worth learning by heart. To put plain text into rhyme and metre is easy ; not so to write a passage which every time it is remembered shall suggest a new train of thought, a new subject of delighted dream.   It is this mystic secrecy of beauty which is the seal of the highest art, which only opens itself to close observation and long study.

I have been ten years learning to understand Turner—I shall be as many more before I can understand Raphael ; but I can feel it a little in all first-rate works.   The Apollo never strikes at first, nor the Venus ; but hour by hour, and day by day, the mystery of its beauty flushes like life into the limbs as you gaze ; and you are drawn back and back for ever—to see more—to feel that you *know* less.

Now, all this, remember, is *general.* As regards my own poems, believe me, I do not think that they *must* be fine, if they are incomprehensible. I only say that their obscurity is not to be urged as at once damnatory, not until it can be shown to be an affected mask of commonplaces. And pray do not, because I have sent you *two* sheets of self-defence, give me up as a hopeless offender. I am rather fond of quarreling — arguing, that is — and perhaps, sometimes persist in it when I am undecided in my own opinion, for the sake of an argument; but you will find that it *is* possible to convince me, and when I am once thoroughly convinced I shall confess it. You have only found three faults, and two of

those in one couplet. I know that
there are hundreds you might fix upon ;
and if you ever look at the things
again, and will tell me what you notice,
believe me, I shall be obliged : for,
though I shall never touch these things
again, having written them all in fatigued
moments and without thought, I shall
know what to guard against in future.

Once more, forgive me for this in-
fliction ; you see what an unlucky thing
it is to set people off on their hobby—
and don't talk any more about imper-
tinences. Remember me most kindly
to all your family. My father and
mother join in kindest regards to yourself : my mother reads all your letters
and says she hopes they may do me
good, she is sure they ought ; so am I.
—Ever most truly yours,

J. RUSKIN.

VIII.

MY DEAR C——

"B.," but my last letter was two-sheeted; and, candidly, I was a little afraid of boring you by another too soon; besides, I have not been particularly well. Things went wrong with me at Albano, two months ago, and I have been very lazy since — blood coming three days running, and once afterwards; better now, however, and delicious weather here, so that I can do anything and go anywhere, at any time, in any dress, and in the fresh air all day. After a thorough spell of drawing, I have put up my pencils—rather sulkily, by-the-bye : for this place is quite

beyond everybody but Turner—and sit
down at the eleventh hour to answer
your enquiry, "Can you tell me anything of Peterborough?" In the hope
of your requiring no information on the
subject, under the probability of your
having already got more than I can
give, I need not reply at much length.
Of the town, whether lively or dull,
pleasant or pestiferous, I know absolutely nothing. The Cathedral is the
most original and bold in conception of
exterior (or rather of west front) of all
our English basilicas; it is very corrupt — and very impressive — throughout. I think, from what I remember,
the services are well performed; the
cloisters are beautiful, though ruined;
the churchyard the most beautiful in
England. Altogether, I think I would
rather have it for a study than any

other I remember ; the town looks cheerful, but the country round is dead flat. I should think there were no walks, and a good deal of marsh hydrogen.

I have just read your letter over, which leaves me in a very uncomfortable doubt of your being in any particular point of space, and possessed of an exceedingly indistinct notion of your state of existence, as you date from three places and profess an intention of going to two more. I shall take you up at Clifton, and toil after you in vain. I don't wonder at your admiring Clifton, it is certainly the finest piece of limestone scenery in the kingdom, except Cheddar, and Cheddar has no wood. Did you find out the dingle running up through the cliffs on the south side of the river, opposite St. Vincent's ? When the leaves are

on, there are pieces of Ruysdael study
of near rock there, with the noble cliff
through the breaks of the foliage, quite
intoxicating; but I cannot endure the
Avon—(*Mantua, May 20th.*)—nor the
wells, nor the fashionabilities, nor the
smoke, nor the boarding-schools on the
downs, nor the steamers on the river,
nor any other of the accompaniments.
I had much rather be with you—where
you go next—at your uncle's house in
Yorkshire (Is this synonymous with
" Copgrove "?)

There you get metaphysical, and on
a stiff subject, too—natural affections;
you ask if this coldness (towards
unseen relations) be peculiar to *you.*
Certainly not ; nor do I think it
can possibly be peculiar even to you
and me.   I think the *instinct* of the
human race is as much below that

of lower animals here as in other cases. We cannot fish out our relations by the smell, as sheep or cows could; nor should I be much disposed to believe in any stories of instinctive clinging towards an unknown relative. But why should you think this "selfish"? It would be much more selfish if we loved a certain number of human beings merely because they have so much of *our own* flesh and blood in them, than if, as seems generally the case, we gave our affection under the gradual influence of mutual kind offices. In the one case, the relation is loved with a selfish love, as part of ourselves: "This is *my* son, sir." In the other he is but treated with pure justice and gratitude as our benefactor, or with that strange but beautiful affection given to those whom we have benefited.

It seems to me that, as far as mere theory goes, the claims of relations *as such* upon our good offices are totally untenable and unjust to the rest of mankind. But such a principle never can be carried into practice, because, though people would be glad enough to cast off their relations if public opinion permitted it, it would be odds if anybody else were a bit the better for it. Still, it is odd that the domestic affections, founded as they are in our most trivial habits, unjustified in nine cases out of ten by any worthiness of object, and bestowed with as little concurrence of our reasonable nature as a cat's love of its native hearth, should be such ennobling, dignified, beautiful parts of our moral system.

Who would not scorn—and that justly —a man who had no patriotism? Yet

what is patriotism but an absurd preju-
dice, founded on an extended selfish-
ness? Who would not detest a man
who should weigh his brother's request
as if it came from an utter stranger?
Yet how is it just that a worthier claim
should be rejected, because habits of
sitting in opposite chairs have brought
the affections together?

It is not a subject to be pressed however; for an affection, however unreason-
ably placed, is always a good thing, and
our fault is not that we love our relatives
too much, but that we do not include all
who live in the number.

That theory of Lord Dudley's about
association has been held by quantities
of people, I believe, but in its extreme
it is of course mere nonsense. It has
arisen, I suppose, from people finding it
difficult to give just reasons for their

deriving more pleasure from one object than from another, the attempt to do so being primarily as reasonable as an attempt to assert logical causes for our preferring otto of roses to asafœtida. Numbers of pretty fancies may be formed about the thing; numbers of them may be secondarily and locally true; but you must have a good, down-right brutal instinct to begin with, or you never know where you are. God has said, "You shall like this, and you shall dislike that," and there is an end of the matter; it will be liked and disliked to all time, though all the associations in the world stood in array against the impulses. On these natural feelings one may set to work; one may teach, accustom, associate, and do a great deal to increase, diminish, or change, but the natural instinct is still the source of all.

You may well ask, what does Lord Dudley mean by association? it is a very ambiguous word. I should not allow your pleasure in looking at a path which Rob Roy had trodden to be the result of association: it is a legitimate historical interest. You do not think the stones, or the grass, one bit the prettier for it; and therefore, as far as it affects your notions of beauty, the association is void. Still less should I allow seeing God's power in the great deep to be association: it is actual observation of interesting fact. But suppose that during some particularly pleasurable passage or moment of your life your eye falls unconsciously on some stick or stone of particular form, and that, years afterwards, you see another stick or stone resembling it, you would instantly feel a thrill, a sensation of sudden beauty in

the inanimate object, which you would
not be able to account for to yourself or
anybody else ; you would kick it and turn
it upside down, and say it was an odd
stone, and you never saw such a stone
before, and you could not tell what was in
the stone, but it certainly was a beautiful
stone.   This illegitimate connection of
ideas is, I think, what theorists mean, or
ought to mean, by association, and it
operates to a vast extent on all our sensations, so much so that I suppose not
one of our tastes is entirely free from it.
But it would take an infinite deal of
association to make me like brown better
than red, though you were to seal all
your letters with brown wax henceforth
for ever.

It might seem degrading our emotions of beauty to bring them down so
completely to instincts, but as all our

admiration of natural objects is of course resolvable into admiration of colour, form, and size, with that of power and motion occurring at intervals, it would seem to be just.   It seems to be sometimes permitted us to trace the purposes of God in giving us these instincts —as painful sensations are generally destructive, and pleasures the contrary ; and in our sensations of beauty it would seem that a healthy mind has a natural attraction towards, and admiration for, attributes of material things, which are illustrative of the attributes of the Deity. All composition is, as you know, based on our love of three in one. A picture must have three centres of colour, three of shade, three of light, and these three must be so united as to form one.   All fine forms of nature, in hills, leaves, branches — what you will — are triple.

Seven seems another number connected with Deity. So you have the seven colours of the lens, resolvable into *three*, forming one pure light by their union. So you have the seven notes of the gamut, resolvable, I believe, into three. So you have the triangle as the first and simplest of all forms—and so on. But all this is mere speculation, mere curious coincidence, perhaps meant to show us that there was a meaning in our instincts, but not in any degree elevating those instincts—pure, unmanageable, downright instincts they always must be.

I am exceedingly sorry to hear of your sister's illness ; but I am not sure that you need therefore regret the want of your carriage. In my own case I never found the slightest benefit from carriage exercise. It seems to·shake the nerves about, but does not stretch a muscle.

Motion of the arms seems to be the most thoroughly [1] one can take ; but it is tiresome for an invalid, especially when, as in your sister's case, perfect exercise of limb and body cannot be taken. Probably the cough was owing in a great degree to this terrible winter. If May is proportionably warm with you, as with us, I hope it may be entirely gone.

I am not, as I told you, much better myself.   Hitherto the climate relaxes most abominably, and all exertion becomes fatigue; but I am now getting fresh air all day—and all night, almost—and am doing better.   We hope to get over the Alps in about a fortnight, if they are safe ; but there is much snow on them, and the avalanches are very dangerous at present.   However, we [1] come straight home, as straight as roads will

¹ (Spaces left where the paper was torn under seal.)

go, and ['] fast as I can come—not above
forty miles a day that is—so there will be
full time for you to let me know the
result of the Merton election, and any
other matters about yourself; and don't
be afraid of *details*, as you call them—
a letter never reads kind without them.

I don't know what I shall do when I get
home. I cannot read, nor take my degree, nor have I much cause so to do for a
year or two, as I can undertake no duties.
I was thinking of getting some small
place in Wales for a laboratory, and to
hold my minerals, among the hills, where
I could have a poney (? pony) and grow
my own cabbages ; and then you must
come and stay with me, and plan rooms
and put up bookcases together. It would
be very nice, I think ; but I have got
quite out of the habit of looking forward

¹ (Spaces left where the paper was torn under seal.)

to things, for I never know one day whether I may not be incapacitated from everything next morning. And everything disappoints one so desperately as you get up in age. That power of being happy with a few violet-seeds or foxglove-bells is so glorious in childhood— so severe a loss, no prospects of men can ever recompense it. Ambition disturbs, science fatigues, everything else cloys. Not but that I can sail a boat in a gutter or build a bridge over a rivulet still, with much delight and self-edification ; but one does not like to look, even to one's reflection in the water, so like an idiot. Senses of duty and responsibility too are confounded bores. What a nice thing it was at six years old to be told everything you were to do, and whipped if you did not do it ! One never felt that one had got such a nasty thing

as a conscience rustling and grumbling
inside. I find nothing equal to quiet
drawing for occupying the whole mind,
without fatiguing one of its powers. I
have got a decent number of sketches,
forty-seven large size and thirty-four
small, but even then my eyes hinder me.

I have found nothing in all Italy com-
parable to Venice. It is insulted by a
comparison with any other city of earth
or water. I cried all night last time I
left it, and I was sorry enough this time,
though, of course, I have lost the childish
delight in the mere splashing of the oar
and gliding of the gondola, which assisted
other and higher impressions. I got well
over the Doge's palace this time, into
every hole and corner of the prisons,
over the Bridge of Sighs, into all the
secret chambers of the Council of Ten.
It looks now as if there had been a

slight proportion of what one would call gammon about it. The prisons are unpleasant enough, chiefly because, lying under water, they have no daylight and not much air ; but, for mere upholstery, I should not suppose a cell of Newgate much better. They are little dens of about 8 feet by 6, 6 feet high, cased with wood, with a wooden immovable bench by way of bedstead ; one circular hole, four inches over, to admit air. The chambers of torture are pretty well lighted—they are at the top of the palace ; but as all the black hangings are gone, and have been succeeded by plaster walls of a merry cream colour, they produce no very terrific effect. This is the most thoroughly stupid town of Italy. Verona is glorious—Florence a bore—Rome a churchyard—Naples a Pandemonium—Paestum a humbug.

I have got your soap, and I shall send it you as soon as I get home. But I hope, in spite of your warning, to receive another letter before then; but don't bore yourself, if you are busy about your election. The kindest remembrances to Mrs. C—— and all your family. Ever your most sincere friend,

J. RUSKIN.

IX.

53 RUSSELL TERRACE, LEAMINGTON.

(*My future address till further notice.*)

September 27 [*Postmark*, 1841].

MY DEAR C——

Your kind letter of the 18th with its dissertation on the duties of correspondence puts me into a very particular quandary. For after a great many generalities about sensible and useful letter-writers—and very proper resolutions to drop all who are not sensible and useful in all they say or write—you ask me pointedly whether I think this a correct line to draw. To which query, if I give a definite answer, you may turn round upon me with an " Out of thine own mouth will I judge thee," and vow

you will have nothing more to do with
anybody writing such a cramped hand
and so much nonsense. Wherefore all
I can say is, that if you keep me you
may cut as many other people as you
like ; and if you cut me your principles
are radically wrong. You say chit-chat
on both sides is wrong. Would it be
wrong to rest yourself in conversational
chit-chat ? and is the stroke of the pen
so very laborious as to render that
which from the tongue is recreation,
labour from the fingers—to make what
would be innocent in sound, criminal in
sight ? Are there not many five minutes
in the course of the week when an
instant's odd feeling might be noted
down, a perishing thought arrested, a
passing " castle in the air " expressed—
with much pleasure to your friend, and
perhaps some even to yourself ?   I

rather think that the choice of our
correspondents should be referred rather
to our feelings of pleasure than of duty.
If I think a person can sympathise
with me in a stray feeling I have
pleasure in communicating it ; and more
in doing so on paper than by words,
because I can do it more completely.
Therefore I do not look to my correspondence as a duty to be performed, but
as the very best mode of entering into
society, because one talks on paper without ever uttering absolute truisms to fill
up a pause, without ever losing one's
temper, without forgetting what one has
got to say, without being subjected to any
of the thousand and one ills and accidents
of real conversation. Therefore if I like
a friend at all, I like him on paper.
And to say I will not correspond with
a person is just the same as saying I

will not know him more than I am
compelled to do. This is going very
far—but I hate society in general. I
have no pleasure, but much penance, in
even the *presence* of nine out of ten
human beings. Those only I like to be
with, whom I like to write to—and *vice
versâ*. I think, therefore, when you say
that you cannot conscientiously correspond with people, it is much the same as
saying you cannot associate with them.
For surely time is generally ten thousand times more wasted in the commonplaces of the tongue, than in selecting
such pieces of our mind as would be
glad of sympathy, and folding them in
the sheet of paper for our friend. I
don't think it ought to be labour. You
should learn to write with your eyes
shut, and then it is mere exercise of the
right hand.

You ask me if I am thinking about my degree. If my health continues to improve I shall go up for a pass next Easter. Jephson says he will make me perfectly well; he has made me much fatter already—or, to speak more correctly, less lean. Chest I think a little better; altogether I am under no anxiety.

I am sorry to say I know absolutely nothing of entomology. I have a great respect for the science; but I always thought it a disagreeable one in practice, partly from the constant life-taking, partly from the concatenation of camphoric smells which one's collection constantly exhales, and partly because—to make any progress—a constant dissection and anatomising must be gone into, really as laborious and half as disgusting as any transaction at Surgeons' Hall. I was much tempted to begin botany among

the ruins of Rome, but I found it did not
suit my eyes at all, and gave it up.
I find quite enough to do with the
sciences necessary to geology. Chemistry and fossil ichthyology are
enough for a lifetime in themselves.
Do you know, I don't remember recom-
mending any political life of Burke.
Nor do I think such a thing has been
produced by any friend of mine. You
had better think over your acquaint-
ances, lest you pass the real recom-
mender thankless by.

You ask me if I would not prefer
notes often to letters seldom. I don't
know. Notes are always half filled up
with dates and signatures and formula.
But if, without wasting time on any such
rubbish, you will write on pleasantly
and easily to yourself, and as the bits
are done send each off—a thought now

and a thought then, with E. C. at the bottom and no "my dear J.," nor hopes of anything, nor remembrance to any-body—then I should most certainly prefer hearing often of you to getting a double sheet once a twelvemonth. Remember, however, that the notes are the actual losers of time in folding, sealing and posting. Still I am not sure that I should not be the gainer by it, for unless you keep your long letters by you, and write a bit now and a bit then, there will certainly be less in it than in the aggregate of notes.

I am a sad fellow for new books—I see very few. Alison's " History of Europe"[1] has an over-reputation at present. I am reading it, and find it verbose and inconsistent with itself in opinions and arguments. But as a statement of

---

[1] (Cf. " Modern Painters," vol. ii.—ED.)

facts I should think it excellent. There were several things I had to say I haven't said, but I will write again soon. Sincere regards to all your family.

Ever most truly your friend,

J. RUSKIN.

X.

MY DEAR C——

I did not answer your *note*, because I wanted to have gone over to Twickenham first; and I did not instantly answer your *letter*, because I was very much vexed at finding I was too late, and because I wanted to look over your letter carefully before answering it. It was in the main much what I expected; and as you say you dislike reasoning on these subjects, I will say no more, especially because I think I have no right to run the risk, in asking for light from others, of extending my darkness in any degree to them, which I might possibly do even to the firmest faiths, without deriving equivalent benefit. But I will ask you two more questions: 1. Do you think that there is any chance for part of mankind of dying altogether—of annihilation, as so far supported by that text—"They who shall be accounted worthy to obtain the resurrection from the dead"—and some others? 2. If you do not believe this, do you really believe in an eternity of extreme bodily and mental torment for nine-tenths or some such proportion of mankind?

Your letter is very unsatisfactory in one respect—that it does not tell me anything about anybody, except that "*they* are gone to Cheltenham for the winter," which, however beneficial it is to be hoped it may prove to the ladies included in the pronoun, is not particularly pleasant news for *me*. Is all your family gone? and how are they? and how are you? and what have you been idling at Twickenham for? how much leave of absence have you?

I don't agree with your *note* (never acknowledged) in its eulogium on horses. I can't endure them; they are the curse of England, and make horses of half our gentlemen. They are very good sort of things for devil-may-care, simoomy blackguards of Ishmaelites to make friends of, or steaks of—as the case may require; but for civilised creatures like us to risk our necks and brains upon, too bad. There's Karslake: he would really draw well if he didn't like horses; but he never gets hold of a piece of paper without covering it with indelicate rumps and cocky tails, and runs the risk every day of his life of terminating his earthly career in a ditch, with an affectionate series of friends to— leap over him. A cowardly, ungenerous brute too, taking instant advantage of a weak rider, and never behaving decently but when it can't help it. Horses indeed! They are not even useful on paper. A cow is good for something; a stag, a crow, a sheep, a goat, a goose, anything but a horse, will do people good when they get into a scrape in composition; but anything equestrian is ruin. Don't talk to me about horses.

It is late, and I am obliged to take so much exercise that I have hardly any time for letter-writing. I am studying with Harding too for foliage, and he gives me a great deal to do; but I suppose I can be of no further use to you, you have cut all these things. Must I, when I follow you?

Remember me most kindly to all your family when you write. Send me at least a note when you can. All here join with me in kind regards.—Ever most truly yours,

J. RUSKIN.

XI.

[The outside sheet of a letter
bearing *postmark Dec.* 22, 1841].

You ask me for some *bold* things in pencil to copy. If *chalk* will answer your purpose, I will send you some fragments of Harding (under whom I am hard at work on foliage now), which are worth five thousand of anything of mine; and if you want materials I will get them sent you. These bits are only *trees*, however, and ground; if you want architecture, I must try my own hand. Pray do not give up your drawing; the great use of it is, that it enables you to seize and retain thousands of ideas which would otherwise escape you, merely by their picturesqueness.

Depend upon it, it raises the mind as much as it recreates it.

I am exceedingly glad to hear of your sister's returning health, after her late severe trial. I hope the severity of this winter, early set in as it is, will not throw her back. Are you going to stay at W—— all winter? I shall wait to hear from you before sending the drawings, as though they are mere scraps and boughs on odd corners of paper, I should not like to lose them. You will receive herewith, I hope, a copy of F. Off[g][1] for next year, of which I crave your acceptance, and, if you ever condescend to such light work now, critical perusal.

Remember me to all your family, and

---

[1] (" Friendship's Offering " for 1842, containing " The Last Song of Arion " and " The Hills of Carrara." Cf. " Poems of John Ruskin," published in complete form in 1891.—Ed.)

with kindest wishes of the season for them and you, believe me, ever most truly yours,

J. RUSKIN.

I send your sermon back by this post.

XII.

DEAR C——

Looking over my letters to-day, I came across your questions, which with shame I recollect *not* to have answered. You *must* have a holder for your chalks—

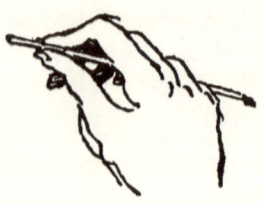

though you should often take them this way, pinching [1] between your thumb and two first fingers, but letting it go clear through your hand. You should also

---

[1] The point of the second finger is seen below the thumb; it therefore touches the chalk with the hollow of its uppermost joint.

place your paper upright, as on an easel, in sketching, and sketch holding your pencil exactly as you would a foil or broadsword. This will give you a feeling and *touch*, so to speak, all *up your arm*. You may use common writing-paper to practise shading or separate touches, *per se*, as mere exercise of hand, but you must not attempt copying except on proper paper : we have quite enough difficulties to contend with without making them.—Ever yours.

J. R.

XIII.

[*Postmark, February* 21, 1842].

MY DEAR C——

You really are a very good boy. I
have not got so nice a letter from you
this year past, and was afraid you were
losing your spirit, getting dull, or blue,
or lazy, or ill; but this last is quite satis-
factory, and so I send you back a leaf
of your sermon which, having accident-
ally dropped out as I was packing it up,
and remained undiscovered till the rest
was posted, has been thenceforward de-
tained by me, in hopes you might *miss*
it (as I heard an omnibus cad remark
to an old lady the other day as he
picked her bag up out of the straw:
" P'raps, marm, if you don't take it

with you you'll miss it "), and send after it, and I might thereby get a letter out of you.

What do you mean by your post-script? To whom *should* I write if not to the only one of my friends whom I cannot see? I made very few at college, most of them above my sphere of life, and therefore necessarily lost as soon as I left. Acland I see every now and then; and he is fifty times worse than you at answering, for I never got but two decent letters out of him, and you—before you had something better to do—sent me many.

Why do you say you have no ideas in common with me? I should be very sorry for my own sake if such were the case; and if it *were*, it would only render our letters more useful to each other and, according to your own principle,

I

render correspondence something like a duty.

Why do you call yourself "indolent?" It is one of the last faults I should have thought of in you. My impression of you has always been as of a person of singularly active, *somewhat* changeable, energetic, and cheerful disposition. I never remember seeing you idle or disposed to be so for a second, and I am certain that an indolent person *could* not possibly have been so unvarying in their sweetness of temper. Idleness or indolence always makes people morose ; while I never remember seeing the spring or the gentleness of your mind fail. I must have a talk with you about it some time.

I am busy enough just now, and shall be, for these two months, hardly able to write to anybody. I believe I shall go

up to Oxford somewhere about April-
Fool Day—by way of doing things con-
sistently—as the examinations begin on
the 15th, and I want to be a fortnight
with Mr. Brown before they begin. I
should be glad if I could see you at
Herne Hill first; for you, by your own
account, and I, without doubt, shall be
plagued enough at Oxford.

I am glad you like the drawings, as
far as they go; they are things which
you can take up for five minutes and
drop again (in copying), in a convenient
way for a busy life. By-the-bye, notice
that your paper has *two* sides, and draw
on the smooth one. If, when you are
tired of everything else, you will just
take up your çhalk and a bit of waste
paper and cover it with this sort of
thing, endeavouring to get the shade at
once, clear and *even*, not blacker at one

part than another, with a broad point,
you will always be making progress;
changing the direction, as at *a*, makes it

look more flexible.   When really applied
to foliage, you can do it with your eyes
shut, as it is a mechanical habit of hand
that is wanted.

Thank you for taking my impudence
about your sermon so good-naturedly.
I should almost be glad to be what
you call me—a private judgment man—
rather than the *nothing* I am ; but I find
it so intolerably difficult to come to
any conclusion on the matter, that I

remain neither one thing nor another. Both extremes, I feel certain, are wrong, but where or how to fix the mean I know not. Whom to believe implicitly—whom to pay respect to—whom to dispute with—whom to judge—I cannot tell; never can attach any real practical meaning to the word "church." Does it mean my prayer-book—or my pastor—or St. Augustine? or am I *generally* to believe all three, and yet dispute particular assertions of each? One thing only I know—that I had rather be a Papist than a dissenter—or a member of the Church of Scotland; and I think the error of blind credence is error on the right side, but it *is* an error for all that; and when to stop, or why to stop, or how to stop, in belief of interpretation or teaching, I cannot tell. I have not time to write more. I did not mean to object to your statement—that Christ was to judge the *whole* world—but to express some wonder at your implied suspicion of our believing that he was only to judge *half* of it.

I have not said half I had to say (no more impudence, however), but I am bothered with this degree; I can't write Latin—I am nervous. I am very glad to hear all your family circle have escaped the winter well. I don't think I can get to Twickenham before I go to Oxford, but shall wait on them instantly on returning.—Ever most truly yours,

J. RUSKIN.

XIV.

[*Postmark, March* 12, 1842].

MY DEAR C——

You are better than good.[1] I had no hopes of another letter so soon ; mighty pretty too ; many thanks. But I haven't time for a word, except just to express my obligations for the bit of George Herbert, whom I think I shall bring out some day in an illuminated missal form, all gold and sky blue, as he ought to be — the most heavenly writer I know.

To answer about shade. The two

---

[1] (This sentence is erased in the original, and the following paragraph inserted above:—" I kept this two days, expecting to see you. As you haven't come I send it, only erasing my first too favourable expression of opinion."—ED.)

great requisites in shade are : first,
" evenness," that is, that one part of
it shall not be irregularly or accident-
ally darker than another, but that it
should be quite flat and equal, for this it
always does in nature ; and, secondly,
"transparency," which means that it
should look (in a tree) as if you could
fly *through* it if you were a bird,
or (in anything else) as if it were
something not laid *on* the object, but
between you and it, *through* which you
saw it.

Now, so that you secure these two
qualities, it matters not in the least what
means you secure them by ; only, the
less the means are visible the better is
the drawing, because the *means* of nature
are *never* visible ; that is, in a mass of
shade, you cannot distinguish or arrange
the individual touches of shade (as in

leaves) by which it is produced. But
you will soon find that if two touches of
chalk cross each other they are darker
together than separately ; if,
therefore, you produce your
shade thus :
(supposing each of the groups of ink
strokes to represent one broad chalk
touch) you will have your shade darker at
the intersections than between them, and
thus lose *evenness ;* therefore, the lines
must not pass over one another, though
they should often touch.   If, again, you
leave no white paper between, you lose
transparency, the interstices of the foliage, and, therefore, you must be able
to arrange touches so as never to
cross or interfere with each other, and
yet to touch and separate irregularly and
playfully as leaves do.   Now it is found
by experience that the means most

calculated to produce this impression are touches of this kind:

very badly done, by-the-bye, for there was a hair in my pen, which has blotted, and so lost the very thing most wanted, evenness.

These touches are susceptible of great change of character, in shortness, sharpness, character of. extremities, individual breadth of line, &c., according to the tree you want ; but the great thing to be noticed in them is, that if one be sharp

and black it will not unite, or be in harmony with another, but
will be like a discord in
music, unless all are of
the same *tone* and cha-
racter or, at least, changing gradually.

Now, at *first*, the more
regularly and symmetric-
ally you can do your
shadow thus, so that all
the points *a*, *b*, *c*, *d*, will be
in one line, that line itself bending like
foliage, by-the-bye, and so
on, and each line at exactly
the same distance from its
neighbour. My step at *e*,
being too big, spoils the
whole. The sooner, I say,
you can do this, the sooner will you be able
to conceal all this artificial mechanism,

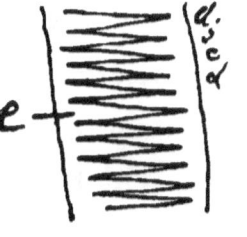

and let your pencil run about the
paper as carelessly as Nature herself,
quite sure it cannot do wrong, for this
regularity is not *visibly* present in good
drawing, the best drawing of all being
that in which you can least tell what has
been done, or how it has been done ; in
which you cannot distinguish touches, or
say where the pencil touched paper first
and where it left it ; those drawings, in
fact, which it is physically impossible to
copy touch for touch.

But it is not till you have acquired the
power of producing this perfect symmetry

of shade that your hand is to be let
loose to do what it likes. So in out-
line you must begin thus—plague take
it, I can't do it to-night—try again.

But all this mechanism is afterwards to
be loosened, and mixed up, when your
hand gets used to it, and to become

&c., even this being twenty times too
symmetrical to be right. But I can show
you more with the chalk in your hand
in five minutes than thus in an hour,
for the pen will not give my meaning ; so you must come and see me.

I hope I shall have seen you, indeed,
before you get this letter. If I don't,
I will send another in a rage after it.

Meantime, my mother's kind regards —governor travelling—mine to all at Twickenham. Forgive this scrawl—I am very sleepy. Ever yours,

J. RUSKIN.

XV.

[The outside sheet of a letter.
bearing *postmark*, *August* 19, 1842].

I have also spent, as I suppose almost everybody has, much time in endeavouring to *colour* before I could draw, and to produce *beauty* before I could produce *truth*. Luckily, there was always sufficient *work* in my drawings to do my hand a little good ; and I got on—though very slowly—far enough to see I was on the wrong road. The time was wasted, but did not do me *harm*. Now I hardly ever touch colour—never work from imagination—and aim so laboriously at truth as to copy, if I have nothing else to copy, the forms of the stones in the heaps broken at the side of the road. Now therefore I am getting on, and look forward to ultimate power and success.

But all this does not apply completely to your case. If your other engagements put it out of your power to make consistent effort, if you are hopeless of going so far as to have your reward, do not waste the few moments you *have* upon the grammatical work, of which *quantity* is required before it will pay. Ten minutes a day, or say a quarter of an hour, regularly and severely employed when you get up, or before dinner, or at any time when you *must* be at home, would ensure progress and power ; but if you cannot do this, better give your hour a month to amusement. Make it as pleasing as you can to yourself ; for it would do you no real good, however directed. I cannot understand even a Prime Minister's being

so busy as not to be able to have a little
table and closet or corner, with all his
things lying constantly ready in their
places. No putting away and taking out
again, mind; and sitting down at quarter
to eight every morning, and getting up
and going down to breakfast at eight—
always locking yourself in, and never
talking to anybody, nor thinking of anything else at the time. And where so
little time is given it ought, if possible,
to be early in the day; otherwise the
hand may be shaky and the mind dis-
tracted—especially with clergymen, or
any persons obliged to pass through
serious scenes of duty. I do think that,
if you are punctual with your meals,
you would never feel the quarter of an
hour, either just before or just after
breakfast, as any loss to your day.

I fully agree with you, that the success

K

of your present desultory efforts should encourage you, and induce you to consistent ones, as proving a certainty of their being rewarded ; but it should not make you think you can do without them. Even supposing you to succeed to the utmost of your expectations, yet you never would gain any certain knowledge of Art. You would be perpetually in doubt and indecision respecting what was really right or wrong —liking one thing one day, another another—a state very different from the gradual dawn and determination of fixed principles, which day by day rise out of your practice, and prop you for further effort. The delicious sensation of a new truth *settled*, a new source of beauty discovered ; for the consequence of real progress in art is never that we dislike what we once admired, but that

we admire what we once despised, and
that progress may always be tested by
the power of admiration increased, the
capacity for pleasure expanded.

Time was (when I began drawing) that
I used to think a picturesque or beautiful
tree was hardly to be met with once a
month ; I cared for nothing but oaks
a thousand years old, split by lightning
or shattered by wind, or made up for
my worship's edification in some particular and distinguished way. *Now*,
there is not a twig in the closest-clipt
hedge that grows, that I cannot admire, and wonder at, and take pleasure
in, and learn from. I think one tree
very nearly as good as another, and
all a thousand times more beautiful
than I once did my picked ones ; but
I admire *those* more than I could then,
tenfold.

Now this power of enjoyment is worth working for, not merely for enjoyment, but because it renders you less imperfect as one of God's creatures—more what he would have you, and capable of forming—I do not say truer or closer, because you cannot *approach* infinity— but far *higher* ideas of His intelligence. Whether, to attain such an end, you cannot, by a little determination, spare a quarter of an hour a day, I leave to your conscience.

I had a great deal more to say, but it would be merciless to cross such a hand as mine.

We arrived here this morning, having come back by the Rhine from Chamonix, where we stopped a full month, with infinite benefit both to body and mind. Lost a little in ill-temper at the muddy, humbuggy, vinegar-banked

Rhine, but very well on the whole. I will write as soon again as I can, but shall be rather busy at home for a month or two. Remember me respectfully to Mrs. C—— and all your circle. With best wishes for the renewal of your sister's health, believe me ever most truly yours,

J. RUSKIN.

XVI.

[*Postmark, September* 19, 1842].

MY DEAR C——

I had intended being beforehand with you, as my last letter was rather a complaint than a chat, but I have to thank you for your last, even though it is a little unruly. And so, because it doesn't suit you to do precisely what is *right* in art, you will do nothing. You won't draw at all, because you *ought* to finish your sketches if you did. *Do* finish your sketches, in the name of all that's industrious. Many an hour have I wasted over half-work, which I didn't like, which would have been profitable had I spent it in my own way; but I denied myself the pleasure, and yet dawdled over the work, and so lost both play and profit; and thus your conscience is too delicate to admit of your doing what you like in drawing, but not too delicate to let you do nothing at all. Finishing your sketches will do you a great deal of good, in mechanical matters—though I very much doubt the expediency of finishing, unless the very day or hour after the sketch has been taken. To forget a thing is better than to be deceived in it; and it is better that your sketches should tell you a *little* truth, than a *great deal* of falsehood. It is better that they should be feeble in verity than distinct in deception. However, I believe you will take your own way at last, and so it is no use talking.

I have not seen the book you speak of, but if it praises Turner *unqualifiedly* you may trust to it.

I think, judging by my own feelings, you were very right in refusing the vicarage. A clergyman's life in a crowded parish seems to me the most dangerous to health and life, and the most replete with every kind of annoy-ance, of any other state of virtuous life. If you are comfortable where you are, $\frac{2.00}{14.00}$ is not the sort of portion which should induce a change ; but I don't think many men would have been so prudent.

Do you do nothing but divinity now ? have you no varying pursuit ? What books are you reading ? Do you botanise at all ? it is surely a clerical science, if there be one in the world. I don't think, by-the-bye, in your chemi-cal question at end of last letter, you have stated the facts correctly. I don't think that a more rapid loss of caloric takes place in mutton than in beef, but that the point of *congelation* is higher. Dip your thermometer into the gravy at freezing-point, and if it determines a lower temperature, we will farther consider of it ; but be particular that the quantity of carbon developed by the cook in the form of what people commonly and irrationally call " brown " be equal in both the joints, as this circumstance will very much affect *radiation.*

When may I hope to see *you* ? I believe I shall be in town now for a year—really quiet—perhaps for two, as we are going to change our house in a fortnight ;[1] and I intend to try some experiments in the way of flower effect. People usually consider flowers as

---

[1] (Reference to the removal from Herne Hill to Denmark Hill.—Ed.)

individual pets, and not as coloured media, by which a landscape may be artistically affected—"aff" or "eff," whichever you like : and when I have got my gentians and violets into proper *tone*, you must come and criticise.

I got really rather fond of flowers at Chamonix, for there nature uses them as I say—not to deck a bank, but to paint a mountain.

I intended to have sent you a drawing as you desired me, on the 8th, but couldn't find *one* fit.

Accept my kindest wishes, in which all join. I fear I shall not be able to get over to Twickenham for some time, being in a bustle with moving, and busy besides with art, chemistry, and a little Greek.—Ever yours,

J. RUSKIN.

WAS THERE DEATH BEFORE ADAM FELL, IN OTHER PARTS OF CREATION?

I. IT is always to be remembered that geologists, and, generally, the asserters of the existence of death previous to the Fall, appeal not to any text of Scripture for *proof* of their assertion—they affirm only that Scripture leaves the matter entirely undecided; and that therefore they are at liberty to follow out the conclusions to which they are led by *other* evidence. Hence, when it is allowed that such and such a text "can neither prove nor disprove" anything relating to the question, they have all that they contend for.

I did not therefore bring forward the text, Rom. viii. 22, as in any way *proving* what I asserted, but because I have heard it over and over again used on the *other side*, as a proof that all animals were affected by the curse on Adam.

Now, what Miss C—— says, that the word *ktisis* is used of the animal creation in other places, is quite true; but there is a peculiarity in the use of the article before it, in this verse, which limits it to man. The first and pure sense of this word is "the *act* of creation," in which sense it is opposed to *ktisma*, which means "a thing created." In this its pure sense *ktisis* occurs *without* the article in Gal. vi. 15, in which verse it is carelessly translated in our version "a new creature," which turns the verse into nonsense; the right sense being "neither circumcision availeth &c., nor uncir &c.," but new birth—new creation.

The opposing word *ktisma* occurs in

1 Tim. iv. 4, of meats; in Rev. v. 13, viii. 9, of beasts; and in James i. 18, of all created things.

The word *ktisis, without* the article, occurs with the meaning of creation generally—creation of the world—in Mark x. 6, xiii. 19; Rom. i. 20; and 2 Peter iii. 4.

From this sense it slides gradually into that of a created thing—as we say a beautiful *creation*, of a flower or other created object. So it occurs, Rom. viii. 39; 2 Cor. v. 17; Col. i. 15, and Heb. iv. 13; in all these cases without the article.

It is used, however, *with* the article in Rev. iii. 14, where the article is made necessary by the following words: "of God,"—not "creation" generally, but *the* creation *of God*, which is to distinguish it from that universal creation of which God the *Father* is said to be πρωτότοκος first-born, Col. i. 15, where no article is used ; but *Christ* is in Rev. iii. 14 said to be, not the first-born of *all* creation, but the beginning of *the* crea- tion *of God.* (And *we* again are said to be the ἀπαρχή, first-fruits or tribute, not of creation, but of the lower word *ktisma*, James i. 18.) *Ktisis* is again used with the article in Rom. i. 25, where the article is rendered necessary by its op- position to *the* Creator.

I am aware of no other passages in which the word occurs with the article, except Mark xvi. 15, Rom. viii. 19, 20, 21, 22, and Col. i. 23. In these in- stances the article is used with singular force and constancy, πᾶσα ἡ κτίσις, αὐτὴ ἡ κτίσις, πάσῃ τῇ κτίσει &c.; and in all these cases its sense is absolutely limited to man, *the* creature of creatures, the chief creature of God.

Hence it is that I say, we have no right whatever to draw any argument from our translation of Rom. viii. 22, as if it included the whole creation ; for in that verse the word is in the original peculiarly and closely limited to man.

II. The power of reproduction involves the necessity of death in many ways. First, because God never gave power without necessity for its use. If the trees first created on the earth were to be imperishable, there was no necessity for a power in them of creating others. The world would have been called into existence in perfection at once, as many trees and animals might have been created as would exist in perfection and happiness together, and all the complicated apparatus of fructification dispensed with. God never makes anything more complicated than is necessary, nor bestows a faculty without an object.

Secondly, the light little parenthesis of Miss C——, "provided there be sufficient nourishment," begs the whole question. The farmer cannot grow wheat twice running in the same field, because *one* crop entirely exhausts the silicate of potash necessary to the existence of the plant. Nor will it grow again until the *death* either of the plant itself (as in straw used for manure), or of some other plant containing the same salt, has restored it to the soil. The sapling pine cannot rise to its full growth, nor, indeed, to *any* growth, until the *death* of its parent has restored to the soil its carbonate of potash. We may imagine a tree maintained for ever in full strength without demand upon the soil; but the moment we hear of its bearing seed, that moment we know that it must perish. Its seed implies that God has willed it to have a successor. Its successor cannot rise but out of its decay.

But it is not merely the death of *plants* which is implied by the *growth* of plants. They require in all cases an element for their growth, nitrogen, which they can only assimilate in one form, *ammonia;* for no chemical means, however powerful, can cause the combination of nitrogen with any other element but oxygen, unless it be presented in the form of ammonia.

It is accordingly found that *no* plants can grow unless supplied with ammonia; and they can be supplied with ammonia in one way only—by *animal* putrefaction. There is no ammonia in the soil; there is none in the decayed remnants of vegetable matter. It exists in the plant only

L

in the crude and unripe juices; in the perfect plant, it exists separately as hydrogen and nitrogen, and cannot be assimilated by its successor. There is, therefore, only one source from which the plant can derive it, the atmosphere; but there is no ammonia in the atmosphere except what results from animal decay. All the nitrogen of animal matter is given off, on its decay, as ammonia. This ammonia combines in the atmosphere with the carbonic acid, which is the result of animal *breath*. The carbonate of ammonia so formed is dissolved in rain water, and presented in this form to the root of the plant.

We, again, require for our nourishment, not ammonia, but the nitrogenised substances, gluten, albumen, &c., of plants. Hence, each species of existence furnishes in its death food to the other, and the nourishment of one implies the simultaneous dying of the other.

Nor is it ammonia alone which the plant takes from the animal. Carbonic acid, also a product of decay, as well as of breath, is its staple nourishment—not more essential than ammonia, but required in far greater quantity. *We* are machines for turning carbon and oxygen into carbonic acid ; the plant is a machine for turning carbonic acid into carbon and oxygen. Hence the plant is the supplement of the animal, and the animal of the plant.

Hence a balance must be kept between them ; if either exceed its limit, it must perish for want of the other ; and the inorganic constituents of the earth are left in a state of perpetual circulation from death to life, and *vice versa*.

Hence, whenever we talk of life,

nourishment, or increase, we talk in the same breath of a supplementary death and diminution.

Nor were these laws otherwise in Eden. The green herb was to be for *meat*. This was destruction. Was it *less* destruction because violent and sudden? or did it less imply capability of decay, than if we had been told that the trees died themselves? We might as well say that the death of Abel did not imply capability of death in man.

And, finally, let us suppose for a moment that all these laws of nourishment and creation were suspended, and that there was sufficient matter for assimilation in the soil to supply *all* plants, multiply as they would, and sufficient nitrogen so prepared to nourish all animals, multiply as they would; and suppose death impossible.

In two centuries after the creation the earth would have been packed tight with animals, and the only question remaining for determination would have been—which should be *uppermost.* Long before the flood the sea would have been one solid mass of potted fish, the air of wedged birds, and the earth of impenetrable foliage.

And let us not suppose for a moment that geology has opened to us worlds different in organisation or system from our own. It has but expanded before us the vast unity of system, the *one* great plan of progressive existence, of which we form probably, the last link. The plants of past ages have the same organs, the same structure and development, as those growing now ; none but the practised botanist can tell the leaves from each other. The animals played precisely the same part in relation to them ; their organisation was the same as now, their ranks of destructive existence appointed in the same order. A few extraordinary (to us) creatures existed, peculiarly adapted for certain circumstances, but in no essential points, in nothing but outward form and strength, differing from their modern types. The digestion of the Ichthyosaurus is as regular and simple as that of any living aquatic beast of prey, and far more easily traceable. Even size is no unfailing characteristic. No fossil fish has been discovered fit to hold a candle to our modern sharks or whales, though the shark tribe was infinitely more numerous than it is now ; but there were too many, and they kept each other thin. It is a curious fact, by-the-bye, though well known, respecting the beneficial influence of the carnivora even on the animals they prey upon, that if you stock a fish-pond with carp only, at the end of a year or two you will find all your fish miserably thin and have no more weight of fish (if you drag the pond) than you put in. But if at first you put in with the carp a few pike, say one in four, you will, when you drag your pond, have twice the weight of carp, in good condition, and all your pike into the bargain.

I see that Miss C—— objects that the growth of plants is not sufficient for animals as it is. Locally, it is not. Universally, it is far too great for them. Our farmers may rise the price of corn over a county, but the Great Forest stretches its uninhabitable growth over America, for the space of a thousand kingdoms. And even where vegetation is limited, this is simply because the plants are not fed by their own *death;* for though they have the animal *volatile* products of ammonia, &c., they have *not* the fixed salts except when they are laboriously restored in the form of manure.

With respect to the question respecting the naming of fish, I can only reply in the words of the questioner, that all such speculations lead us only into a labyrinth. There are thousands of difficulties connected with the Mosaic account. What, for instance, does *Eden* include? For the *garden* was *in* Eden, and eastward in it. And was man, supposing he had stood, never to have left his primal and narrow nursery-and-seedsman sort of habitation? How, if so, could he "replenish the earth and subdue it"? Was the same trial to be sustained by all? And how could it be sustained, unless gardens and trees of knowledge were multiplied over the earth as the population spread? &c. &c.

The whole appears to me, but for the close geographical account of the Garden, very much like an Eastern allegory; but however that may be, I think it is better always to read it without reference to matters of physical inquiry, to take the broad, simple statements of creation—innocence, disobedience, and guilt—and then to take in equal simplicity of heart such revelations as God may deign to give us of His former creations, and so to pass back through age before age of preparatory economy, without troubling ourselves about the little discrepancies which may appear to start up in things and statements which we cannot under-stand.

Creation may have been suspended in its functions for a moment—for the half-hour (divines seem to think it was little more) of man's probation. It matters not to us. What we are we know—and what we may be, we know; what we have been, God knows.

There is much of mystical in Scripture, which, doubtless, will one day be made manifest; but we do but waste our lives and peril our faith by trying to unravel it before its time. We shall not break the seal by dashing it against stones.

I have said, I see, that *no* ammonia exists in the atmosphere but what arises from the putrefaction of animals. This is not strictly true, for several mineral springs supply it in considerable quantity; not enough, however, in all the springs of Europe, to feed the vegetation of Lombardy for half a year.

Supplies of this kind are probably proportioned to the gradual increase of animal life, and consequent demand for more nitrogen. The immediate acting supply is deduced only from animal corruption. From every churchyard, from every perishing remnant of the life of the forest and the sea, rises the constant supply of carbonate of ammonia, which feeds the green leafage of spring, and expands the pulp of the bright fruit.

Liebig says that the source of this ammonia is sufficiently evident by its peculiar odour, if rain water be evaporated with a little sulphuric acid, and then tested with lime.

On the other hand, while the supply of ammonia is gradually, very slightly, but still certainly on the increase, that of carbonic acid is much diminished. Immense quantities of this acid existed formerly in the atmosphere, which fed the colossal vegetation of geological eras. By that vegetation it was gradually withdrawn; and, animal life not being sufficiently extended on the earth to feed on this vegetation, and so return the carbonic acid to the atmosphere, it was withdrawn for ever; its oxygen was restored by ordinary vegetable action, making the atmosphere purer for the abode of man, and its carbon deposited in the enormous coal-fields, which are now the source of all his vastest powers. Animal and vegetable life are now better balanced. The vegetable, having no extraordinary supply of carbonic acid, is diminished in growth; and the animal feeding on this diminished growth restores the carbon to the air, and provides for the equal growth of the succeeding plant.

XVII.

[*Postmark, January 8,* 1843].

MY DEAR C——

Many thanks for your kind letter and enclosure, which I have read very carefully, and like exceedingly—especially the concluding part of it, which is very graceful and impressive ; nor, on the whole, do I think you are at all wrong in taking advantage of the popular notion respecting the Fall, as it is too essential a part of most persons' faith to be lightly struck at, nor unless under very strong convictions of some necessary or important truth which it prevents the reception of. But when you are thinking of the subject yourself, for your own private edification and

good, I wish you would tell me what
is your notion of a *tree*.

You will most likely have a conception
of a thing with leaves on it, and bringing
forth flowers in its season. You cannot
conceive a tree without leaves and
flowers. Now what do you mean by a
leaf and flower ? You mean by the first,
an instrument for depriving carbonic acid
of its oxygen, and giving carbon to the
plant. You can have no other meaning; for leaves are of all colours, and
forms, appearances, and have nothing
in common but this—this is the essence
of a leaf. You mean by the second, a
part of the plant which has in it organs
of fructification. You can have no other
meaning but this ; for flowers have no
common form, nor appearance, nor anything essential but this.

Therefore, you mean by the first,

something which is perpetually giving to the plant that which it had not before ; and by the second, a preparation for the production of another plant. You imply, therefore, growth—change of state — and preparation for a succeeding existence. Therefore, when you say "a tree," you mean a growing, changing, and preparing thing.

Now it cannot grow for ever, for then there would not be nourishment for its substance. Whatever stops its growth must be a loss of energy in the vital functions—that is, incipient death. When you say a growing thing, therefore, you mean something advancing to death. Neither can the new tree and the old tree exist together. One must perish to make room for the other. Therefore, every bud and blossom of the parent tree implies and necessitates its destruction.

Therefore, when you say a preparing thing, a fructifying thing, you mean a *dying* thing. Therefore, whenever you speak of a tree, you speak of death. That which has not in it the beginning and germ of death, is not a tree. Consequently, if there were trees in the Garden of Eden there was death ; or, if there was not death, they could not have had leaves, nor flowers, nor any of those organs of growth or germination which now constitute the essence of a tree. People will look very grave at you, indeed, if you hint that there were no *flowers* in the Garden, and yet the very meaning of the word flower is—something to supply *death*.

But if you can suppose that Scripture tells you that there were trees in the Garden, and means in saying so something which had neither leaves nor

flowers, nor any organs of a tree, you
may give up your trust in the whole
of it at once; for you can never tell, if
there be such latitude of interpretation,
what anything *means* throughout the
book. Therefore, either Scripture is
wholly to be distrusted, as meaning one
thing when it says another—or there
was death in Eden.

Again: what do you understand by
the term "lion?" Surely an animal
with claws and sharp teeth. If it have
not claws and teeth it is not a lion,
it is some other animal—a different
animal from any that we have any
notion of, but not a lion. But if it have
claws and teeth, do you suppose God
gave it claws and teeth for nothing?
The gift of an instrument supposes the
appointment to a function. The claw
is to catch with, the teeth are to tear

M

with, and there is a particular juice in the stomach to digest meat with. Now to suppose that these were given without intention of being used, is the same thing as to suppose that your tongue was given to you without your being intended to talk or taste with it, and that it is by corruption of nature that you walk with your legs. A lion at peace with other animals is therefore a contradiction in terms—or at least it is the same thing as saying that God has adapted every muscle to a function which it was never intended to discharge. And though by special miracle the lion shall eat straw as the ox, that does not prove that it was made to eat straw, any more than the miracle of Elisha proves that iron was intended to be lighter than water—which, if it were, the whole economy of the world must be changed.

Hence, if these animals were at peace in Eden, they were either created with especial view to their *after* functions, and maintained for a short time at peace by especial miracle; or else they were different animals—not lions nor tigers, but things of which we have no conception, having different muscles, no claws, no digestive organs for meat, &c. &c. To the first of these positions, the naming by Adam gives the lie direct, for it implies knowledge of their nature; and how could Adam know their nature, when every one of their functions was miraculously suspended? The second position is more possible, partially implied by the speaking of the infant, but yet it supposes a *new creation* at the fall of Adam, which I cannot but think would have been at least indicated in some way or other in Scripture.

Further. By the institution of carnivora, one third more *happiness* is brought
into existence. For the earth will only
by its appointed constitution feed a certain number of herbivora; and by making
them food to a higher series, one more
step of existence is gained.

Further. There is not *one* text in
Scripture, out of which you can squeeze
the slightest evidence that death did not
take place with the lower animals.

Wherever death is mentioned as coming by man, the resurrection is mentioned
as parallel with it. If you suppose the
doom extended to the animals, so must
the recovery be. In the expression,
"The whole creation groaneth and tra-
vaileth," &c.—the words are πᾶσα ἡ κτίσις,
precisely the words used to the apostles ·
when our Lord bids them preach the
gospel : πᾶσῃ τῇ κτίσει. Do you suppose

our Lord meant to bid them preach to the *whole creation* ? No—but the other text is falsely translated ; it can only mean " Every man—all men—every creature groaneth," &c.

Further. All this evidence coming from the visible, present creation, and Scripture, we have, in addition, geological evidence of death extending for an infinite series of ages before man. Lyell has discovered the bones of the mastodon, the most recent of all fossils, in a bed *cut through* by the ancient course of the Niagara, three hundred feet above its present bed, and three miles and a half below the falls ; in cutting back from this point, the river by the very lowest calculation must have been occupied 15,000 years.[1] My own conviction is, therefore—it don't much

[1] (*Cf.* Lyell's " Principles of Geology," ch. xiv.—ED.)

matter what it is, but I believe it is most
people's who pay any regard whatsoever
to modern science—that man in Eden
was a growing and perfectible animal ;
that when perfected he was to have been
translated or changed, and to leave the
earth to his successors, without pain.
In the doom of death he received what
before was the lot of lower animals—
corruption of the body—and, far worse,
death of the soul.   I believe the whole
creation was in Eden what it is now,
only so subjected to man as only to
minister to him—never to hurt him.
The words "to dress it and keep it"
speak volumes.

The only passage in your sermon
I didn't like is that about tradition.
Why say that is based on tradition
which you can so easily prove from
Scripture ?

It is late. Remember me to all at Twickenham. I am very glad to hear your invalid is at least no worse.—Ever yours affectionately,

J. RUSKIN.

XVIII

[*Postmark, Feb.* 7, 1843].

MY DEAR C——

I think your last apology as un-
founded as your first was unnecessary,
and I think you had much better try no
more. I should have answered your letter
a month ago, if I had known what in the
world to say to it. Don't write me any
more such stuff—and, above all, measure
yourself rightly. It is quite as wrong,
and as far from anything like real
humility, to underrate as to overrate
ourselves; and to say, when you are
working very hard in the noblest of all
professions, that you are hiding your
talents under a bushel, is not giving

God credit nor honour for the grace He has given you.

As for the major part of your letter, it is very beautifully expressed and felt; and that bit of glorious George, which to my shame I have not repeated to myself, nor thought of for a year or two (though I never forgot a word of it from the first moment I cast eyes on it), is a clincher. But yet it requires the preaching of a considerable deal of patience, to make one sit out some of the sermons I speak of, comfortably; not, observe, because I go, as you think, to be *amused* or *tickled* by speculation or oratory. I go, I hope, to receive real benefit of some kind or another; but then how am I to be benefited? Not by the bare rehearsal of duties which I know as well as my alphabet; not by the repetition of motives which are constantly before me,

and which I never act upon ; not by
the enunciation of truths which I perpetually hear, and never believe. But
by giving explanation to the duties,
force to the motives, proof to the facts ;
and to do this in any degree requires
some part or portion of intellect above
mine, or *different* from mine; and
when I find this, I get good—otherwise
not. I can conceive how different the
feeling of a really religious person might
be, and how each trivial expression
of the minister might raise in their
minds some pleasant thought or new
devotional feeling; but even then I
should fancy that the following words
of the preacher were as likely to be an
interruption, as an assistance to the train
of thought he had previously awakened.

To-day being the first Sunday of the
month, Mr. Melville preached at the

Tower, and his curate gave us a sermon
on "Unto Adam also, and to his wife,
did the Lord God make coats of skins,
&c." "Now," thought I, when he
began, "I know what you're going to
say about that ; you'll say that the beasts
were sacrificed, and that the skins were
typical of the robe of Christ's righteous-
ness, &c.—that's all of course ; I wonder
if you can tell me anything more." Well,
he began : "As by sin came death, there
could be no death before sin." "Ah,"
thought I, "it's a pity you don't know
something of natural history ; it's not
much use my listening to any more
of that, because we haven't common
premises to start from, and I shan't
believe a word you say."

Nevertheless, I did listen, and got—
diluted into three quarters of an hour—as
much as I knew about the text, and no

more, save and except a charitable wish
on the part of the preacher—" *May* we
all be clothed with this robe," &c.
"What the deuce," thought I, "is the
use of your stupid wishes? do you
suppose people don't usually wish for
all that's good for them, though they
don't take a quarter of an hour to say
so?" So much for the benefit I got
from my sermon.

I am glad to hear you are reading Sir
Joshua Reynolds; it is very good sterling
matter, though it is not well arranged,
and not very *recherché* or original.
You will find *Fuseli's* and *Barry's*
Lectures worth a great deal more; the
former especially, being an accomplished
scholar, unites art and literature, and
rather gives you the philosophy of the
fine arts as a group, than the techni-
calities of any one. He is peculiarly fit

to be studied by men who only make painting a subservient and recreative part of their occupation, because he shows its connection with other subjects of the intellect. Both he and Barry are deep thinking and original. Sir Joshua's reputation depends partly on his popularity as a practical man—partly from the very shallowness of his work, which puts it down to the level of men's idleness. To read Barry or Fuseli requires more thought and attention than people care to be troubled with. But Sir Joshua's is a good book as far as it goes.

I received on Thursday a most kind note from Mrs. C——, asking me to dine there on Friday. I was unluckily out all Thursday, and did not receive my note till eleven at night, so that my answer next day would, I fear, not be in time to prevent their waiting dinner for me.   I could not possibly go, as I expected my father home from a journey ; and I am so much engaged at present that I have not even an evening, much less a day, to spare to my engagements for two months to come.   I should not apologise for this, even though I could help it, for of course the loss is all on my side, and the very first day I have to take my pleasure in, I shall go over to Twickenham.   I hope Miss Blanche C—— has recovered her health; you have given me no reports lately of the health of your family.

Have you ever read Mrs. Sherwood's "Henry Milner"?   I should like to know what you thought of her religion. It is a kind of religion I am particularly fond of, but I'm afraid it's improper. Sincerest regards when you write to all

at Twickenham.—Ever yours affectionately,

J. RUSKIN.

I don't quite know what you mean
by "lithographic boards." I use lithographic paper, but not boards; but I
think chalk or pencil drawings on anything require to be fixed. I use, myself,
plain *milk, boiled* and applied very hot,
only once, as rapidly as possible; but I
never saw a chalk drawing fixed without
being spoiled, and almost prefer leaving
them to take their chance. There are
people in London who fix them, making
it a profession, and do it well; but I do
not know their secret.

XIX.

[Letter mutilated at the beginning].

I was[1]   in Green Street in the
course of last week, to find that you had
given me a wrong statement of time, and
that · Mrs. C——, having stayed only
five instead of ten days in town, had re-
turned to Twickenham the day before.
I hope, however, to be able to get over
to Twickenham soon.

Thanks for your note.   What are you
giving up your curacy for? and where
are you going? and how long may I
hope to see you here?   Write to tell me
concerning[1]

The text, by - the - bye, of the green

---

[1] (Spaces left are where a portion of the letter has
been cut away).

herbs given for meat rather confirms
the geological view than weakens it;
for you see the *fishes* are omitted—
which is as much as an intimation that
then, as now, they were almost entirely
carnivorous, and that the mention of the
green meat given to the earth-animals is
rather an illustration of the bounty of
God in giving that sweetness and soft-
ness to seeds and fruits, unnecessary to
them, and meant especially for the
pleasure and health of animals, than any
limitation of the animals to such food.
Fishes are so entirely dependent upon
their own tribes for food—the ultimate
nourishment of the smallest being
derived from matter (probably in a
state of decomposition) too delicate to
be appreciable—that the very naming
of anything in the shape of a fish,
may almost be received as a direct

N

assertion of existence supported by death of others.—Ever yours affectionately and in haste,

J. RUSKIN.

XX.

MY DEAR DOCTOR,

Allow me respectfully and prophetic-
ally so to address you, and to wish you
a very *profitable* New Year, and as many
of them as may be expedient and proper
for you. Happiness I have no doubt
you despise, so I don't mention it; but
pray convey my best wishes in that
respect to all at Twickenham, only keeping as many for yourself as you consider
perfectly correct.

You are a nice person certainly, to
come to London and back, without so
much as a *sham* call (saying you'll
come, and staying away)—though you
do go through the ceremony on a larger

scale and with grander effect, writing
to ask people questions about their
latitude three weeks before, when it
don't matter to you whether they are to
be at Rome or Richmond, for all that
you intend to make of them. However
I won't scold—they have little enough of
you at Twickenham now—and it would
be a hard case if they had to send you
all the way over here for nothing.

Thank you for the drawings. I shall
call for them the first time I pass.
You may do yourself good even in
working up your sketches—if you put
in all the *accidents* from nature. If you
want a tree, go and look for one that
suits you, and put it in twig for twig;
if you want a bank, a bunch of grass, or
anything that you have hieroglyphised
in the comprehensible parts of your
sketch—as *there* though not represented

—do not attempt to recollect it, but put a *bonâ fide* bit of truth instead.

If you do not do this, every touch of composition is waste of time—worse, it is vitiation of the eye and hand.

No artist can compose with benefit to himself, until his mind be full and over-flowing with the closest and most accurate knowledge of the facts of nature. Above all, don't imagine that what you suppose to be recollection is anything beyond composition. You may remember if a tree sloped to the right or left, if it were tall or short, graceful or grim, slender or stout; but all its details, every one of the important and distinctive features, on which the pleasure with which the reality affected you was mainly dependent, are altogether beyond either your or anybody else's recollection. And the worst and most

careless drawing that you make faith-
fully on the spot, twig for twig, as far as
it is in your power, will be immeasur-
ably better and more beautiful than the
prettiest you can make out of your
head.

Your powers of toleration are magni-
ficently elastic, however. I congratulate
you exceedingly on your mild reception
of what you supposed to be a moon
shining in her own eyes—I have heard
of men standing in their own light, but
I should not venture even to realise that
much of phenomenon in a painting. I
think everything is allowable in an artist
that violates no law of nature, but not
a step further. What you suppose to
be moonlight in reverse is the light of
the western sky, still falling on the
higher parts of the building, and casting
visible (though indistinct) shadows. In

southern countries the light from the
west is often intense and effective for
half an hour after the sun has set (I don't
mean, of course, down to the tropics, but
in the south of France), and casts
shadows and illustrates objects like
actual sunlight — contrasted, of course,
very frequently with deep gloom behind,
which I have here enhanced by dense
clouds so as to give the moon fair play.

I am very glad you like the picture.
As for your saying Turner's trees are
wiggy, you should have a wigging for
it—but you will know better soon.

[*Letter Unfinished*].

XXI.

MACUGNAGA—VAL ANZASCA, *August* 3.
[*Postmark, August* 18, 1845].

DEAR C——

I used to write many and long letters
home when I was abroad formerly, but
then I was lounging—now I am working ; and I usually work myself stupid
by the close of the day, and think it
unfair to give my dregs to my friends.
I assure you I have written only five
letters, except to my father or mother,
since I left England ; and those were
letters promised or of necessity, the
result of which is, that with most people
I suffer not thinking on like the hobby-
horse ; but as I suppose you will still
have some indignant memory of me,

I would fain soften it a little, and get you to send me some talk.

I have not seen an English paper for six weeks, and the last that I saw I didn't read; so it matters not how stale your news is, it will entertain me, more especially as, since I left home, I have received just *two* letters except from home itself. One of those was on such thin paper that I couldn't read it; and the other was from your friend Gordon, which told me that he had got wet, and that he didn't know where he was going next. So that up here among the hills— living in a deal cabin, in which I can't stretch without taking the skin off my knuckles, with not a soul whom I can speak to except the cows and the goats and a black puppy, and some sociable moths who come in the evening to put my candle out—I begin to feel more

like St. Paul or St. Anthony than myself. I don't mean *our* St. Paul, but
their St. Paul here—the first hermit, who
had the two lions to dig his grave, the
two pious lions that wouldn't go away
afterwards till they had got St. Anthony's
blessing.

And another reason of my writing was
that I heard from home you were in
want of a presentation to Christ's
Hospital, and that I fear you will think
it very odd or unkind that we can't
give it you. But mercy on us—though
we haven't many relations, some of
them always contrive to make themselves miserable once in five years ; and
they come to one for muffin caps and
yellow stockings, as if we could bake
the one and dye the other. If you
could but see the letters that come,
three and four a day, for two months

before one has a presentation—there is
enough to make you laugh or cry as
you choose.

Letters from lazy fathers, who don't
like to hear their children squalling.
Fathers *always* say that the young
sprout shows "talent of the most
promising kind," or "far above his
years."

Letters from widowed mothers,. who
always say that they "haven't means
to bring up their children in the
station of *life* they have been accus-
tomed to." The mothers are always
willing to work, one sees that ; they
don't find their children a bore. It
is their confounded vanity that upsets
them ; they can make their shirts and
their shifts, but they can't make 'em
surplices ; and as mothers always want
their eldest sons to have a university

education, and be bishops—and their second son to be Lord Chancellor—and their third, admiral of the blue—they try Christ's Hospital as the first step.

Letters from uncles, which say that their brother was a very worthy man—very much so—but exceedingly imprudent, and they can't support *his* family as well as their own.

Letters from strange ladies, who "have known the family for years, and can answer for their respectability;" and these are exceedingly eloquent, quote texts to an overpowering extent, and promise you as many tickets for Paradise as you want, for yourself and friends, if you'll give *them* one for Christ's Hospital.

I have got two or three letters from the eldest sisters of orphan families, which were the real thing, and very touching—and some very good and sensible ones from aunts. Half-pay officers with eleven children and no wife write in a very dismal tone indeed.

August 5th.—I don't know that the no wife adds practically to the misfortune, but theoretically it does; and they get frightened the first time they have to tuck all the eleven children up.

It is a sin to give you any more of this writing. I write even worse than I did, from scribbling notes on my arm in the galleries. I can't read my notebook except when my wits are at the brightest; otherwise I forget what all the words are.

Will you send me a line—per Billiter Street—and tell me how you and your family are? It's no use my beginning to tell you what I have been about—

merely picture gazing or manufacturing ;
and there are plenty of travels in print
without my sending you mine.—Ever
yours affectionately,

J. RUSKIN.

XXII.

MY DEAR C——

I suppose you must have made quantities of friends at Ceylon, to be able drop your old ones so coolly. For my part, though I can't write to my friends, I never consider them as in the least lost or spoiled by not looking after ; and I think you will find, with people at all good for anything, that it is always so. I feel exactly towards you as I used to do, and was talking of you the day before yesterday. One ought to be able to keep one's friends like one's wine, any number of years in the cellar, and find them only a little crusted at last, and better in flavour than ever.

I didn't answer a note of yours about Christ's Hospital, because I couldn't do the thing—and I thought a letter about a piece of business only, not worth answering.

Tell your sister, with my kind remembrances, that symbolism, although very interesting, and doubtless actual, in creation, is a dangerous plaything; it has wasted the time of the whole of Europe for about two centuries ; and should only be pursued when it is either perfectly plain—or as helpful to the feelings at any given moment when it suggests itself—without being insisted upon as more than a fancy.

Ladies' symbolisms are nearly always sure to be false, from their careless way of reasoning. Thus, in your sister's first idea, she says, "the heart is addressed through the eye and hand." Why

does she miss the ear? Probably because her real meaning was not that the
heart *is addressed*, but *addresses* through
the hand. Nobody is usually addressed
through their hands, except a lover allowed to touch his mistress' fingers for
the first time. We *work* with our hands,
and are addressed through eyes and
ears usually—sometimes through the lips,
I should think—and occasionally by bas-
tinado, through the soles of the feet.

I don't think the doctrine of the Trinity
can be deduced from these premises of
fact. A leaf has two sides, it is true; and
it isn't easy to see how it should have
fewer. But he would be a very doubt-
ful Trinitarian who looked upon the
Persons of the Trinity as its Aspects.

For the trinity of heaven, earth, and
sea, it is a prettier idea; but "the
heaven" is nothing at all—the clouds

are only the sea in another shape—and though the air is a good type of the "Spirit," the "Powers of it" are not supposed to be particularly sacred. Still, the phrase, "born of w. (water?) and of the spirit," in some degree justifies this image ; only if air, earth, and water, are to be a Trinity, what becomes of fire? or oil?—the last as important in its chemical functions in vegetation as water is. All these things *must* be thought over most carefully before a symbolism will hold good.—Always affectionately yours,

J. RUSKIN.

Printed by BALLANTYNE, HANSON & Co.
London & Edinburgh

WORKS BY JOHN RUSKIN.

MODERN PAINTERS. In 5 vols. with all the Woodcuts, 1 Lithograph, and the 89 Full-Page Steel Engravings. The text is that of the 1873 Edition, with all the Author's subsequent Notes, and a New Epilogue. Cloth, 6*l*. 6*s*. the 5 vols., imp. 8vo.

THE STONES OF VENICE. Complete Edition. (Imperial 8vo.) 3 vols. with the 53 Plates and the Text as originally issued, and Index. Cloth, 4*l*. 4*s*. the 3 vols.

EXAMPLES OF THE ARCHITECTURE OF VENICE. With the Text and the 16 Plates as originally published. Cloth cover (unbound), atlas folio (about 25 in. by 17 in.), 2*l*. 2*s*.

THE POETRY OF ARCHITECTURE ; or, The Architecture of the Nations of Europe considered in its Association with Natural Scenery and National Character.

A Prose Work in One Volume of 280 pp., with Chromolithograph Frontispiece, 14 Plates in Photogravure from unpublished Drawings by the Author, and 9 Full-Page and other new Woodcuts. 4to, cloth, 21*s*.

VERONA, AND OTHER LECTURES. Delivered principally at the Royal and London Institutions between 1870 and 1883. Illustrated with Frontispiece in colour and 11 Photogravure Plates from Drawings by the Author. Med. 8vo, cloth, 15*s*.

This volume consists of five chapters, four of which were prepared by the Author to be delivered as Lectures during his tenure of the Slade Professorship at Oxford, and one has been written since his resignation.

GEORGE ALLEN, 156, CHARING CROSS ROAD, LONDON.

ON THE OLD ROAD : a Collection of Miscellaneous Pamphlets, Articles, and Essays (1834-84). In 3 vols., including—My First Editor, Lord Lindsay's Christian Art, Eastlake's History of Oil Painting, Samuel Prout, Sir Joshua and Holbein, Pre-Raphaelitism, Opening of the Crystal Palace, Study of Architecture, The Cestus of Aglaia, Minor Writings upon Art, Notes on Science, Fiction, Fair and Foul, Fairy Stories, Usury, Home and its Economies, The Lord's Prayer, An Oxford Lecture, &c. 8vo, cloth, 30s. the 3 vols. (Not sold separately.)

ARROWS OF THE CHACE : being a Collection of the Scattered Letters of John Ruskin. With added Preface by the Author. Published chiefly in the Daily Newspapers during the Years 1840-80. In 2 vols. cloth, 8vo, 20s. the 2 vols. (Not sold separately.)

PRÆTERITA. Outlines of Scenes and Thoughts perhaps Worthy of Memory in my Past Life. Vols. I. and II. of this autobiography now ready, in cloth, 13s., 8vo.

FORS CLAVIGERA : Letters to the Labourers and Workmen of Great Britain, in 8 vols. and Index vol. 7s. each, 8vo.

THE ART OF ENGLAND. Lectures delivered at Oxford in 1883. I. Rossetti and Holman Hunt—II. E. Burne-Jones and G. F. Watts—III. Sir F. Leighton and Alma Tadema—IV. Mrs. Allingham and Miss Kate Greenaway—V. John Leech and J. Tenniel—VI. George Robson and Copley Fielding—VII. Appendix and Index. Cloth, 6s., 4to.

UNTO THIS LAST. Four Essays on the First Principles of Political Economy. Ninth Edition. Cloth, 3s.; roan, gilt edges, 4s., 12mo.

SELECTIONS FROM RUSKIN. 2 vols. small post 8vo. (Sold separately), cloth, 6s. each; roan, gilt edges, 8s. 6d. each.

THE FIRST SERIES (from Works written between 1843 and 1860), with engraved Portrait after George Richmond's Picture, and an Index, 540 pp.

THE SECOND SERIES (from Works written between 1860 and 1888), with Photogravure Portrait, from a recent Photograph, and an Index, 500 pp.

FRONDES AGRESTES. Readings in "Modern Painters." Twelfth Edition. Cloth, 3s. ; roan, gilt edges, 4s.

WORKS BY JOHN RUSKIN

Crown 8vo, cloth, 5s. each; roan, gilt edges, 7s. 6d. each.

SESAME AND LILIES. A Small Complete Edition, containing the Three Lectures, "King's Treasuries," "Queen's Gardens," and "The Mystery of Life," with long Preface and New Index.

MUNERA PULVERIS. Six Essays on the Elements of Political Economy. Second Edition, with New Index.

The EAGLE'S NEST. Ten Lectures on the Relation of Natural Science to Art. Third Edition, with New Index.

TIME and TIDE, by WEARE and TYNE. Twenty-five Letters to a Working Man of Sunderland on Laws of Work. Fourth Edition.

The CROWN of WILD OLIVE. Four Essays on Work, Traffic, War, and the Future of England. With Articles on the Economy of the Kings of Prussia. Eighth Edition, with New Index.

QUEEN of the AIR: a Study of the Greek Myths of Cloud and Storm.

The TWO PATHS. Lectures on Art and its Application to Decoration and Manufacture. Delivered in 1858-59. With New Preface and Added Notes.

"A JOY FOR EVER" (and its Price in the Market). The Substance of Two Lectures on the Political Economy of Art. With New Preface and Added Articles. Third Edition, with New Index.

LECTURES on ART, delivered at Oxford in 1870. Revised by the Author, with New Preface. Fifth Edition.

The ETHICS of the DUST. Ten Lectures to Little Housewives on the Elements of Crystallisation. Seventh Edition.

The ELEMENTS of DRAWING. In Three Letters to Beginners. Illustrated.

The STONES of VENICE: Selections for the Use of Travellers. 2 vols. cloth, 5s. each. Fifth Edition.

*Small post 8vo, cloth, 7s. 6d. each; roan, gilt edges, 10s. each,
complete with all the Plates.*

The SEVEN LAMPS of ARCHITECTURE.

1. The Lamp of Sacrifice—2. The Lamp of Truth—3. The Lamp
of Power—4. The Lamp of Beauty—5. The Lamp of Life—
6. The Lamp of Memory—7. The Lamp of Obedience.

The 14 Plates for this Edition have been specially prepared from
the larger Work.—Fourth Edition.

ARATRA PENTILICI: Seven Lectures on the

Elements of Sculpture. With 1 Engraving on Steel and 20
Autotype Plates.

VAL D'ARNO. Ten Lectures on Art of the Thirteenth

Century in Pisa and Florence. With 1 Steel Engraving and 12
Autotype Plates.

ARIADNE FLORENTINA. Six Lectures on Wood

and Metal Engraving, and Appendix. With 4 Full-Page Fac-
similes from Holbein's "Dance of Death," and 12 Autotype
Plates.

LECTURES on ARCHITECTURE and PAINTING.

Delivered at Edinburgh in November, 1853. With 15 Full-
Page Illustrations drawn by the Author.

"OUR FATHERS HAVE TOLD US:" Sketches of

the History of Christendom. Part I. The BIBLE of AMIENS.
With 4 Steel Engravings and Plan of the Western Porches of
Amiens Cathedral. Cloth, 6s., 8vo.

ST. MARK'S REST. The History of Venice, written

for the help of the few Travellers who still care for her Monu-
ments. Cloth, 5s., small post 8vo.

MORNINGS in FLORENCE. Being Simple Studies

of Christian Art for English Travellers. Third Edition. Cloth,
4s., small post 8vo.

GEORGE ALLEN, 156, *CHARING CROSS ROAD, LONDON.*

www.ingramcontent.com/pod-product-compliance
Lightning Source LLC
Chambersburg PA
CBHW030108030726
47498CB00007B/2292